"If you are looking for a succinct, ma... introduction to the phenomenon of wo... Ryken has managed what few others in ...ormed tradition could do. He argues for the ubiquity of worldview thinking while respecting the balance between its intellectual component and its most basic attribute: love. And all of it is based on the biblical account of creation, fall, and redemption and its implication for all of life, from the arts, to education, to politics and family life. Required reading for everyone from the educated layperson to students, Christian leaders, and gatekeepers."

William Edgar, Professor of Apologetics, Westminster Theological Seminary, Philadelphia

"Philip Ryken thoughtfully explains the ins and outs of a Christian worldview, backed by considerable biblical support and key selections from cultural touchstones. The book is a quick read but is certainly not slight. Thorough and accessible, this is a perfect resource for students who need a solid grounding or a fresh reminder of truths of the Christian worldview."

D. Michael Lindsay, President, Gordon College; author, *Faith in the Halls of Power*

"I have written a behemoth of a book of nearly four hundred pages on the history of the worldview concept. Philip Ryken, Wheaton's fine and gracious president, has said what needs to be said about a Christian worldview in a much shorter space. And he's said extremely well what needs to be said about it. His book is most engaging. It is, indeed, a privilege to commend and to recommend this magnificent volume. To all: *Tolle Lege*—Take up and read!"

David K. Naugle, Chair and Professor of Philosophy, Dallas Baptist University

CHRISTIAN WORLDVIEW

RECLAIMING THE
CHRISTIAN INTELLECTUAL TRADITION

David S. Dockery, series editor

CONSULTING EDITORS

Hunter Baker
Timothy George
Niel Nielson
Philip G. Ryken
Michael J. Wilkins
John D. Woodbridge

OTHER RCIT VOLUMES

The Great Tradition of Christian Thinking, David S. Dockery and Timothy George

The Liberal Arts, Gene C. Fant Jr.

Political Thought, Hunter Baker

Literature, Louis Markos

Philosophy, David K. Naugle

CHRISTIAN WORLDVIEW
A STUDENT'S GUIDE

Philip Graham Ryken

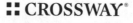
WHEATON, ILLINOIS

Trade paperback ISBN: 978-1-4335-3540-6
PDF ISBN: 978-1-4335-3541-3
Mobipocket ISBN: 978-1-4335-3542-0
ePub ISBN: 978-1-4335-3543-7

Library of Congress Cataloging-in-Publication Data

Ryken, Philip Graham, 1966-
[What is the Christian worldview?]
   Christian worldview : a student's guide / Philip Graham Ryken.
      p. cm. (Reclaiming the Christian intellectual tradition)
   This writing project began with a 2006 booklet entitled What is the Christian Worldview? I am grateful to P&R Publishers for the permission to revise and expand that booklet for inclusion here.
   Includes bibliographical references and index.
   ISBN 978-1-4335-3540-6 (tp)
   1. Christianity—Philosophy. 2. Christian philosophy. I. Title.
BR100.R95   2013
230—dc23   2013021338

Crossway is a publishing ministry of Good News Publishers.

VP		26	25	24	23	22	21	20	19
17	16	15	14	13	12	11	10	9	8

To the memory of
Arthur F. Holmes
who taught me the contours of a Christian
worldview in Philosophy 101

CONTENTS

SERIES PREFACE

RECLAIMING THE CHRISTIAN INTELLECTUAL TRADITION

The Reclaiming the Christian Intellectual Tradition series is designed to provide an overview of the distinctive way the church has read the Bible, formulated doctrine, provided education, and engaged the culture. The contributors to this series all agree that personal faith and genuine Christian piety are essential for the life of Christ followers and for the church. These contributors also believe that helping others recognize the importance of serious thinking about God, Scripture, and the world needs a renewed emphasis at this time in order that the truth claims of the Christian faith can be passed along from one generation to the next. The study guides in this series will enable us to see afresh how the Christian faith shapes how we live, how we think, how we write books, how we govern society, and how we relate to one another in our churches and social structures. The richness of the Christian intellectual tradition provides guidance for the complex challenges that believers face in this world.

This series is particularly designed for Christian students and others associated with college and university campuses, including faculty, staff, trustees, and other various constituents. The contributors to the series will explore how the Bible has been interpreted in the history of the church, as well as how theology has been formulated. They will ask: How does the Christian faith influence our understanding of culture, literature, philosophy, government, beauty, art, or work? How does the Christian intellectual tradition help us understand truth? How does the Christian intellectual tradition shape our approach to education? We believe that this series is not only timely but that it meets an important need, because the secular culture in which we now find ourselves is, at best, indifferent to the Christian faith, and the Christian world—at least in its more popular forms—tends to be confused about the beliefs, heritage, and tradition associated with the Christian faith.

At the heart of this work is the challenge to prepare a generation of Christians to think Christianly, to engage the academy and the culture, and to serve church and society. We believe that both the breadth and the depth of the Christian intellectual tradition need to be reclaimed, revitalized, renewed, and revived for us to carry forward this work. These study guides will seek to provide a framework to help introduce students to the great tradition of Christian thinking, seeking to highlight its importance for understanding the world, its significance for serving both church and society, and its application for Christian thinking and learning. The series is a starting point for exploring important ideas and issues such as truth, meaning, beauty, and justice.

We trust that the series will help introduce readers to the apostles, church fathers, Reformers, philosophers, theologians, historians, and a wide variety of other significant thinkers. In addition to well-known leaders such as Clement, Origen, Augustine, Thomas Aquinas, Martin Luther, and Jonathan Edwards, readers will be pointed to William Wilberforce, G. K. Chesterton, T. S. Eliot, Dorothy Sayers, C. S. Lewis, Johann Sebastian Bach, Isaac Newton, Johannes Kepler, George Washington Carver, Elizabeth Fox-Genovese, Michael Polanyi, Henry Luke Orombi, and many others. In doing so, we hope to introduce those who throughout history have demonstrated that it is indeed possible to be serious about the life of the mind while simultaneously being deeply committed Christians. These efforts to strengthen serious Christian thinking and scholarship will not be limited to the study of theology, scriptural interpretation, or philosophy, even though these areas provide the framework for understanding the Christian faith for all other areas of exploration. In order for us to reclaim and advance the Christian intellectual tradition, we must have some understanding of the tradition itself. The volumes in this series will seek to explore this tradition and its application for our twenty-first-century world. Each volume contains a glossary, study questions, and a list of resources for further study, which we trust will provide helpful guidance for our readers.

I am deeply grateful to the series editorial committee: Timothy George, John Woodbridge, Michael Wilkins, Niel Nielson, Philip Ryken, and Hunter Baker. Each of these colleagues joins me in thanking our various contributors for their fine work. We all express our appreciation to Justin Taylor, Jill Carter, Allan Fisher, Lane Dennis, and the Crossway team for their enthusiastic support for the project. We offer the project with the hope that students will be helped, faculty and Christian leaders will be encouraged, institutions will be strengthened, churches will be built up, and, ultimately, that God will be glorified.

Soli Deo Gloria
David S. Dockery
Series Editor

ACKNOWLEDGMENTS

This writing project began with a 2006 booklet entitled *What Is the Christian Worldview?* I am grateful to P&R Publishing for the permission to revise and expand that booklet for inclusion here—at the generous invitation of David Dockery—in the series Reclaiming the Christian Intellectual Tradition.

A small army of Wheaton College faculty, staff, and students read the original booklet and participated in group discussions about its content. The questions, criticisms, and suggestions of these friends improved my work immeasurably: Chelsea Aldridge, Robert Bishop, Rachael Burlingame, Sarah Carter, Micah Dennis, Jay Fort, Hal Hackett, Sam Hayes, Jonathan Heidengren, Benjamin Holland, Maddie Johnston, Rachel Lamb, Jon Lederhouse, Matt Lundin, Dave McHale, Matt McMillan, Jennifer McNutt, Kelly McSparron, Leya Petrovani, Quentin Rynbrandt, Alan Seaman, and Becky Wilson.

On very short notice, several other colleagues read and commented on the final draft. So I give special thanks to Stan Jones, Jeff Jue, Keith Johnson, Tim Larsen, David Lauber, and Matthew Milliner, as well as to Marilee Melvin and Lynn Wartsbaugh for their help with many practical details in producing the final manuscript.

+ 1

WHAT IS A WORLDVIEW?

Everybody has a worldview. Whether we know it or not, we all have a fundamental perspective on the world that shapes the way we live.

By way of illustration, consider what the following everyday encounters tell us about the various ways that different people look at the world and how they interact with it as a result:

> We are playing baseball at the park, and it's Jack's turn to bat. He's only four, but he knows what he's doing at the plate—better, as it turns out, than he knows what he's doing on the base paths. He hits a sharp grounder back to the mound, which I field and throw to his sister at first for the out. Jack veers sharply away from the baseline and runs haphazardly around the infield before returning to home plate. "I get to choose my own bases," he announces, in what sounds like a basic premise for postmodern ethics. Laughing, I say, "Okay, buddy. You can choose your own bases, but they're not the real bases, so you're still out."

> I am out shoveling sixteen inches of snow into huge piles by the street when a neighbor stops by to speculate as to when (or even if) the snow will ever disappear. "Well, God brought it here," I say, "and only God can take it away." Taking clear objection to my reasoning, my neighbor sniffs, "It was a low pressure system, you know." I did know that, of course, yet I also happen to believe that even the weather system is under God's control.

> Before I move halfway across the country, a friend invites me to his art studio and generously invites me to choose a painting to take with me as a gift. We walk back and forth, admiring his artwork and discussing each piece—where it was painted, how

it is composed, what thoughts and feelings it expresses. Finally, I choose a watercolor depicting a street of row houses from a local city neighborhood. Today the painting has a treasured place in my home, as the memory of a familiar place and a symbol of a valued friendship.

It is two minutes before tip-off in the first round of the playoffs for an intramural basketball league. "Where's Eric?" I ask, referring to our star point guard. "He won't be here tonight. He's leading a high school Bible study." When we lose by four points, we all know that missing our best player cost us a shot at the championship. But we also know that some things in life—such as honoring a ministry commitment—are even more important than basketball.

These everyday encounters all reveal the worldviews of the people involved. What I hang on my wall bears witness to the beauty and truth that Jesus Christ has put into the world. The way I shovel snow is a testimony to what I believe about God's creation and providence. Even the way I play sports reflects the purpose of leisure in an ordered universe.

At the same time, the way other people respond reveals *their* worldview—their faithfulness in keeping a commitment, for example, or their unbelief in the existence and providence of God. Ideas have consequences. Even ordinary interactions reflect our commitments and convictions about the basic issues of art and science, work and play, family and society, life and death. Whenever we bump into the world, our worldview has a way of spilling out. It comes out in what we think and love, say and do, praise and choose.

Worldviews also have a way of bumping into one another. Some of the examples above deal with conflicting commitments at the level of daily life, but of course different views of the world also have culture-wide influence. Some of the major conflicts in today's society—between naturalism and supernaturalism, for example, or between freedom and terrorism, or between purity and promiscuity in popular entertainment, or between abortion and the right to life—come at the intersections where worldviews collide, sometimes violently.

The conflict of worldviews calls Christians to thoughtful cultural engagement. In an increasingly secularized society, the followers of Christ often find their ideas under attack. How can we maintain a Christ-centered perspective on the contested issues of our day? How can we think Christianly in every area of intellectual life? And how can we live out a faithful Christian testimony at home, at school, at church, at work, in government, and in the marketplace of ideas? The answer begins with having a worldview like the one introduced in this book: a consistently Christian worldview that shapes our thoughts, forms our desires, guides our words, and motivates our actions.

DEFINING WORLDVIEW

A worldview—or "world-and-life view," as some people call it—is the structure of understanding that we use to make sense of our world. Our worldview is what we presuppose. It is our way of looking at life, our interpretation of the universe, our orientation to reality. It is the "comprehensive framework of our basic belief about things,"[1] or "the set of hinges on which all our everyday thinking and doing turns."[2] More complexly,

> a worldview is a commitment, a fundamental orientation of the heart, that can be expressed as a story or in a set of presuppositions (assumptions which may be true, partially true or entirely false) which we hold (consciously or subconsciously, consistently or inconsistently) about the basic constitution of reality,

[1] Albert Wolters, *Creation Regained: Biblical Basics for a Reformational Worldview* (Grand Rapids, MI: Eerdmans, 1985), 2.
[2] James Olthuis, "On Worldviews," in *Stained Glass: Worldviews and Social Science*, ed. Paul A. Marshall, Sander Griffioen, and Richard J. Mouw, Christian Studies Today (Landham, MD: University Press of America, 1989), 29.

and that provides the foundation on which we live and move and have our being.[3]

Ideally, a worldview is a well-reasoned framework of beliefs and convictions that helps us see the big picture, giving a true and unified perspective on the meaning of human existence. Alternatively, we could say that our worldview is the story we tell to answer questions like these: Why is there anything at all? How can we know for sure? How did we get here, and what are we here for, anyway? Why have things gone so badly wrong? Is there any hope of fixing them? What should I do with my life? And where will it all end?

Not all worldviews are equally systematic or equally comprehensive. Often there is a difference between the worldview that we think we have and the one we actually live—our functional as opposed to our theoretical worldview. Worldviews can also change according to circumstance. But whether we realize it or not, all of us have basic beliefs about who we are, where we came from, and where we are going. This is unavoidable. Even people who never stop to think about their worldview in any self-reflective way nevertheless live on the basis of their tacit worldview. This is so basic to who we are that usually we hardly even notice our worldview but simply take it for granted. Sometimes a worldview is compared to a pair of spectacles, but, to use another optic metaphor, maybe our eyes themselves would be a better analogy. When was the last time you noticed that you were seeing? We rarely think about seeing; we just see, and we are seeing all the time. Similarly, even if we rarely, if ever, think about our worldview, we still view everything with it. Our worldview is what we think with and ultimately live by.

Many factors contribute to our worldview, not all of them the product of our own thoughtful reflection. In the words of a character from *The Magician's Nephew* by C. S. Lewis, "What

---

[3] James W. Sire, *Naming the Elephant: Worldview as a Concept* (Downers Grove, IL: InterVarsity, 2004), 122.

you see and hear depends a good deal on where you are standing: it also depends on what sort of person you are."[4] Our family background, life experience, economic circumstances, educational pedigree, cultural context, national heritage, linguistic community, physiological characteristics, psychological makeup, and historical situation all have an influence on the way we see the world. Some of these factors are public, not private, which helps to explain why worldviews have so much culture-shaping influence. Worldviews are not merely private perspectives but typically are held in common with other people. This leads the missiologist G. Linwood Barney to compare the relationship between worldview and culture to an onion, with its concentric layers. At the core is a culture's prevailing worldview—its normative beliefs about God, the world, and the people in it. Growing out from that core, there are other layers: values, institutions, customs, material artifacts.[5] All of these cultural layers grow out from a society's worldview or worldviews.

Worldviews are inherently religious. Because our worldview is at the core of who we are, it always reveals our fundamental convictions, including what we believe (or don't believe) about God. There is no spiritual neutrality—no view from nowhere. Even atheists and agnostics direct their lives toward some greater purpose. The theologian Langdon Gilkey wrote: "Whether he wishes it or not, man as a free creature must pattern his life according to some chosen ultimate end, must center his life on some chosen ultimate loyalty, and must commit his security to some trusted power. Man . . . inevitably roots his life in something ultimate."[6] People who say they do not believe in God nevertheless have controlling commitments, which are reflected in how they approach their school-

---

[4] C. S. Lewis, *The Magician's Nephew* (London: Bodley Head, 1955), 123.
[5] Barney's ideas are discussed helpfully in David J. Hesselgrave, *Planting Churches Cross-Culturally: North America and Beyond*, 2nd ed. (Grand Rapids, MI: Baker, 2000), 145. ·
[6] Langdon Gilkey, *Maker of Heaven and Earth: A Study of the Christian Doctrine of Creation*, Christian Faith Series (Garden City, NY: Doubleday, 1959), 193.

work, spend their money, cast their ballots, use their smartphones, and do everything else they do. Whatever is ultimate for us shapes our total identity. "As [a man] thinks in his heart," the Scripture says, "so is he" (Prov. 23:7 NKJV).

Another way to say this is that everybody worships. Human beings are not merely *homo sapiens*—people who think—but also *homo adorans*—people who praise. In an extraordinary address given to the 2005 graduating class of Kenyon College, the novelist David Foster Wallace spoke with astonishing clarity about the centrality of worship (and its consequences):

> There is no such thing as not worshiping. Everybody worships. The only choice we get is *what* to worship. And the compelling reason for maybe choosing some sort of god or spiritual-type thing to worship . . . is that pretty much anything else you worship will eat you alive. If you worship money and things, if they are where you tap real meaning in life, then you will never have enough, never feel you have enough. . . . Worship your body and beauty and sexual allure and you will always feel ugly. And when time and age start showing, you will die a million deaths before they finally grieve you. . . . Worship power, you will end up feeling weak and afraid, and you will need ever more power over others to numb you to your own fear. Worship your intellect, being seen as smart, you will end up feeling stupid, a fraud, always on the verge of being found out. But the insidious thing about these forms of worship is . . . they're unconscious. They are default settings.[7]

The novelist's words carry special force when we read them in the context of his death by suicide just a few years later. What we choose to worship matters desperately and is always bound up with our entire perspective on the world. This is why a worldview can never be reduced to a set of rational propositions. It is a matter of the heart as well as the head—of what we love as well as what

---

[7] Emily Bobrow, "David Foster Wallace, in His Own Words," http://moreintelligentlife.com/story/david-foster-wallace-in-his-own-words (accessed January 4, 2012).

we think. And in the final analysis, the only life-giving worldview is one that leads to the everlasting worship of God.

THE HISTORY OF AN IDEA

The concept of worldview is a fairly recent development in Christian thought. In one sense, of course, the people of God have always had a worldview—a perspective on life that was guided by the Word of God. For Old Testament Israel, that worldview began with a daily confession of faith: "Hear, O Israel: The LORD our God, the LORD is one" (Deut. 6:4). The coming of Christ opened up new dimensions of a biblical worldview. The teaching of Jesus in the Sermon on the Mount, for example, was not so much a code of ethics as it was a new way of looking at the world and living in it. "Christianity is more than a set of devotional practices," writes Robert Louis Wilken in his analysis of the early church. "It is also a way of thinking about God, about human beings, about the world, and history. For Christians, thinking is part of believing."[8] For as long as God has been revealing his truth to his people, he has been shaping their view of the world.

What is relatively new, however, is for Christians to use *worldview* as a central category for thought and life. Briefly outlining the intellectual history of the concept will help us understand what is meant (and not meant) by the *Christian* worldview.

The story begins in Germany.[9] *Worldview* is simply the English translation for the German word *Weltanschauung*, which first appeared in the philosophical writings of Immanuel Kant. Kant used the term as early as 1790, in his *Critique of Judgment* (*Kritik der Urteilskraft*). At first, *Weltanschauung* referred to

---

[8] Robert Louis Wilken, *The Spirit of Early Christian Thought: Seeking the Face of God* (New Haven, CT: Yale University Press, 2003), xiii.

[9] For the history that follows, I am relying heavily on the work of Al Wolters. In addition to his article "World-View" in the *New Dictionary of Christian Apologetics* (edited by W. C. Campbell-Jack, et al. [Downers Grove, IL: InterVarsity Press, 2006]), he has written a useful (though unpublished and incomplete) essay entitled "*Weltanschauung* in the History of Ideas: Preliminary Notes." See also David K. Naugle's definitive work, *Worldview: The History of a Concept* (Grand Rapids, MI: Eerdmans, 2002).

people's sensory perception of the world around them. However, Kant's disciples—the young philosophers Johann Fichte and Friedrich Schelling—adopted the word and began employing it for other purposes. By the first decade of the nineteenth century, *Weltanschauung* was used widely by intellectual giants of German Romanticism and idealism: novelists (Johann Wolfgang von Goethe), poets (Jean Paul), and philosophers (Friedrich Schleiermacher and Georg Hegel). Gradually the term shifted from its literal meaning of sense perception to refer metaphorically to intellectual perception.

In the decades that followed, *Weltanschauung* passed from the poets and philosophers to other cultured communities in Germany. By the 1840s the term had become commonplace among influential musicians (Richard Wagner), theologians (Ludwig Feuerbach), and physicists (Alexander von Humboldt). In a letter to a friend, one historian of the time complained, "Formerly everyone was an ass in private and left the world in peace; now, however, people consider themselves 'educated,' cobble together a 'world-view' (*Welt-anschauung*), and preach away at their fellowmen."[10]

By the end of the nineteenth century, the concept of worldview had taken hold among leading thinkers in other countries. The term appeared so frequently in the titles of books and scholarly articles that the Dutch theologian Herman Bavinck referred to worldview (*wereldbeschouwing*) as "the slogan of the day."[11] The Danish philosopher Søren Kierkegaard was perhaps the first thinker to give this slogan a technical meaning in his system of thought. For Kierkegaard, a "life-view" (*livskanskuelse* in Danish) or "world-view" (*verdensanskuelse*) was the fundamental perspective that undergirded a person's self-understanding and gave unity to thought and action.

Kierkegaard was not the only philosopher to seek a definition

---

[10] Jacob Burckhardt, quoted in Wolters, "*Weltanschauung* in the History of Ideas."
[11] Herman Bavinck, *Christlijke wereldbeschouwing* (Kampen: Kok, 1904), 8.

for *worldview*. Wilhelm Dilthey, Friedrich Nietzsche, Martin Heidegger, and others sought to distinguish philosophy from worldview. Typically the former was identified as an ancient and rational discipline that explored what was true for human thought generally, whereas the latter was more personal and depended partly on one's place in history and situation in life. Of the two concepts, worldview was more perspectival, philosophy more universal. The difference may be illustrated from the thought of two men whose ideas exercised massive influence on the twentieth century: Karl Marx and Sigmund Freud. Their theories of economics and psychology, respectively, self-consciously represented entirely new ways of looking at the world—what the philosopher Ludwig Wittgenstein termed "a world picture" (*Weltbild*).

Meanwhile, some Christian thinkers were adopting the concept of worldview for their own purposes—most notably, the Scottish theologian James Orr and the Dutch statesman Abraham Kuyper. Orr's 1893 book *The Christian View of God and the World* and Kuyper's public addresses at Princeton Theological Seminary (published in 1899 as *Calvinism: Six Stone Lectures*) exercised wide influence on Christian thought. Both thinkers presented the Christian faith as a total view of reality (what Kuyper called a "world-and-life-view") with implications for society as well as the church. Their vision for seeing the world from a Christian point of view has since been carried forward in the United States by theologian Carl F. H. Henry, apologist Francis Schaeffer, prison evangelist Charles Colson, and many others. By the end of the twentieth century, worldview thinking was pervasive in evangelical churches and schools, as Christians sought to integrate learning with faith in every academic discipline and apply it to the central issues of public life.

Perhaps it is not surprising that the concept of worldview has found particular resonance in the church. After all, Christians have a distinctive perspective on the world, and *worldview* serves as a useful construct for explaining why we look at things differently than other people do. Since Christians hold their worldview in common with other believers, it serves as a point of spiritual and intellectual unity. Originally, *Weltanschauung* referred to a person's unique perspective on the world. But for Christians, worldview is less individualistic and more communal. Because it is grounded in divine revelation, the Christian worldview has a fixed reference point in the mind of God, and thus it stands as something that connects all believers everywhere.

This is not to say that Christians agree about everything. Within the general framework of the Christian worldview, the followers of Christ hold a wide variety of perspectives on politics, economics, aesthetics, and many other areas of life and thought. Christians also disagree about doctrine, with different denominations holding distinctive views in theology. Nevertheless, they find substantial unity in the worldview they share. At the same time, there are areas where the Christian worldview overlaps with non-Christian thought. For example, like Christianity, Hinduism holds to the sanctity of human life. Similarly, both Christianity and Judaism teach that God created everything out of nothing. These complexities—both the variety of views that Christians hold and the areas of commonality between Christianity and other religions—prevent us from thinking too simplistically or one-dimensionally about worldviews. But they should not obscure the coherence of the Christian worldview in its basic principles.

Worldview thinking helps Christians engage in the marketplace of ideas. It does this by showing how Christianity relates to everything in life—not just the private life of personal piety but also the public life of art, music, science, business, politics, sports, and popular culture. In addition to providing intellectual perspective for every academic discipline, worldview thinking is useful for apologetics and evangelism. The way people live is always rooted in their religious perspective, even if they claim not to be religious at all. When conflicts arise, as they always do, understanding worldviews helps us identify the deepest source of the conflict and to explain what difference it makes in any situation to follow Jesus Christ.

Admittedly, worldview thinking also has its critics. The German theologian Karl Barth warned that when Christians articulate a *Weltanschauung*, inevitably they reduce the Christian faith to the definite "world-picture" of their own time and place, which is always inadequate.[12] Furthermore, there is always the risk that Christians will use the right worldview for the wrong reasons, exploiting good ideas for ungodly purposes, hijacking the Christian faith for their social, political, or ecclesiastical agenda. There are many examples of this from history, where everything from the medieval Crusades to chattel slavery has been defended on the basis of biblical principles.

More recently, philosopher James K. A. Smith has called for a temporary moratorium on the term *worldview*.[13] His concern is that the worldview approach tends to reduce human beings to disembodied thinkers, when in fact we are embodied lovers. Smith argues that what causes us to act is not only what we know but mainly what we adore. "Before we articulate a worldview," he says, "we worship."[14] In effect, worship is "the matrix from which a Christian worldview is born." So instead of "focusing on what Christians *think*, distilling Christian faith into an intellectual summary formula (a 'worldview')," we should pay more attention to the practices of Christian worship.[15] What will transform us is not information for the mind but formation of the heart through the liturgy of the church.

We can learn from these and other criticisms without

[12] Karl Barth, *Dogmatics in Outline* (London: SCM, 1949), 59.
[13] See James K. A. Smith, *Desiring the Kingdom: Worship, Worldview, and Cultural Formation* (Grand Rapids, MI: Baker Academic, 2009). Another notable critic is James Davison Hunter, *To Change the World* (New York: Oxford University Press, 2010).
[14] Smith, *Desiring the Kingdom*, 33.
[15] Ibid., 11.

jettisoning the vital project of articulating a Christian view of the world. Worldview thinking should be rejuvenated, not rejected.[16] Even if our present grasp of the truth is a work in progress, it is still necessary to defend that truth and live it out as well as we can. We can acknowledge the formative influence of liturgical and other practices without devaluing the intellect. We are rational creatures. While it is true that what we love often shapes what we think, it is also true that the biblical remedy for disordered affections is for God to speak his truth to the mind. "Do not be conformed to this world," writes the apostle Paul. In other words, do not be shaped by the things that this world loves—its patterns and practices. Instead, the apostle goes on to say, "be transformed by the renewal of your mind" (Rom. 12:2). There is an intrinsic, ordered relationship between the thoughts and the affections that guide our actions. The formation of the heart comes through the transformation of the mind. Therefore, one of the primary ways the Holy Spirit changes the things we love and worship is by changing the way we think.

This brings us back to the value of having a Christian worldview—of seeing the world the way that God sees it. But it brings us back with the recognition that people are whole persons. We are lovers as well as thinkers, and therefore a properly Christian view of the world engages the whole person—body, heart, mind, and soul. In developing a properly Christian worldview through the discipleship of the Christian mind, we are growing our capacity for sacred worship and holy love. We cannot be said truly to have a Christian view of the world unless what we love as well as what we think is directed to the glory of God, and unless this is readily apparent in the way we live in the world. The apostle Paul was

---

[16] Smith seems to agree when he responds to his critics by writing, "The argument of *Desiring the Kingdom* is not that we need *less* worldview, but *more*: that Christian education will only be fully an education to the extent that it is also a formation of our habits." See his "Worldview, Sphere Sovereignty, and *Desiring the Kingdom*: A Guide for (Perplexed) Reformed Folk," *Pro Rege*, vol. 39 (June 2011): 15–24.

thinking holistically in his prayer for the mind as well as the heart of the Philippians, which is also a prayer for us in forming and living out a Christian worldview: "That your love may abound more and more, with knowledge and all discernment, so that you may approve what is excellent, and so be pure and blameless for the day of Christ" (Phil. 1:9–10).

WHY WORLDVIEWS MATTER

Our worldview is one of the most important things about us. The English journalist and lay theologian G. K. Chesterton proved this point by using an everyday example: "For a landlady considering a lodger, it is important to know his income, but still more important to know his philosophy."[17]

My own experience confirms the truth of Chesterton's claim. When my wife, Lisa, and I first moved to Philadelphia right after college, we had no money, no jobs, and no income. The day we looked at the beautiful attic apartment that eventually became our home, three other couples were walking through it at the same time. Yet the landlord gave us the lease, almost against his better judgment. I believe his exact words were, "I can't believe I'm doing this, but I'm going to let you have the apartment." Why did he make this decision? Because we had told him that I would be attending a nearby seminary in the fall, and thus he knew our philosophy, as Chesterton called it—our worldview. Even though he was not a devout Christian himself, he rightly concluded from our faith commitment that we would find employment, work hard, and pay our rent on time.

It is desperately important for Christians to have a truly and fully Christian worldview—not just when we go apartment hunting but all the time. Living wisely in the world requires proper perspective. Do we see ourselves and the world around us the way that God sees them, or are we viewing things from

---

[17] G. K. Chesterton, *Heretics*, quoted in Naugle, *Worldview*, xi.

some other perspective? This question is crucial to ask about any worldview. Does our way of looking at the world correspond to the world as it actually is? Do we see the world as it is according to God?

In these post- or hyper-modern times, some people claim that reality itself is plastic, that the universe will adjust to our way of looking at things, that there are as many worlds as there are worldviews. This is not really the case, however, as we discover the moment we try to impose our opinions on other people, or when the difficulties of daily life knock the rough edges off our own particular worldview. The person who says that everyone should have totally unrestrained freedom and the person who says we need to have moral and social restraints cannot both be correct; something has to give. One of my schoolteachers used to say, "Your freedom to swing your fist stops at the end of my nose." Unfortunately, some people believe instead that "might makes right." These two worldviews are incompatible. Sooner or later they will collide, and when they do, it will become painfully obvious that they cannot both be correct.

The English music critic Steve Turner uses delicious irony to criticize the claim that all worldviews are equally valid. His critique comes in the form of a poem—a confession of faith for a postmodern worldview:

> We believe that all religions are basically the same
> At least the one that we read was.
> They all believe in love and goodness.
> They only differ on matters of
> Creation, sin, heaven, hell, God and salvation. . . .
> We believe that each man must find the truth
> That is right for him.
> Reality will adapt accordingly
> The universe will readjust.
> History will alter.
> We believe that there is no absolute truth

Excepting the truth that there is no absolute truth.
We believe in the rejection of creeds.[18]

Turner's poem bears the ironic title "Creed." His point is that people who reject all creeds nevertheless have a creed all their own. The question is: Which creed is correct? Who has the right worldview?

The premise of this book is that the only worldview that fully corresponds to the world as God knows it is a completely and consistently Christian worldview. Unfortunately, it is somewhat doubtful whether most Christians have any very clear understanding of the worldview that belongs to them by the grace of God. One way to demonstrate this is to consider what popular surveys reveal about the way we live. Time and again we are told, to our dismay, that Christians live basically the same way that everyone else lives. We have roughly the same incidence of domestic violence, the same rate of divorce, the same selfish patterns of spending, and the same addictive behaviors as the general population. How can this be true?

When we probe a little deeper, we discover that Christians who are in full agreement with the main principles that undergird the Christian worldview actually *do* live in a distinctively Christian way. To that extent, what the surveys say about the way Christians think and behave is somewhat misleading. But here is the problem: according to one influential survey, only 9 percent of all born-again adults and only 2 percent of born-again teenagers truly espouse the basic principles of a biblical worldview.[19] If people in the church do not think Christianly, it is hardly surprising that they do not live Christianly, either.

The disconnect between what Christians say they believe and the way they actually behave may be illustrated from a provocative comment in a ministry newsletter for Christian men. The newsletter reported, "For every ten men in your church, nine will have kids

[18] Steve Turner, "Creed," in *Up to Date* (London: Hodder & Stoughton, 1985), 138–39.
[19] George Barna, *Think Like Jesus* (Nashville, TN: Integrity, 2003), 23.

who leave the church, eight will not find their jobs satisfying, six pay the monthly minimum on their credit card balances, five have a major problem with pornography, four will get divorced, and only one has a biblical worldview."[20]

The last statistic in this series is the one that explains all the others: only a fraction of Christian men have a truly and fully Christian worldview. If these figures are correct, then the reason so many men fail to provide good leadership for their families, find joy in their daily work, manage their finances well, or resist sexual temptation is that their lives are not totally shaped by the story of salvation, as they would be if they embraced a completely Christian view of the world—not just knowing the Christian worldview but also living it out.

Christian men are not the only ones who have this problem, of course. There are ways in which all of us see the world our own way rather than God's way, regardless of our age, gender, or situation in life. Nor are we the only people who are affected by our failure to live in a consistently Christian way. Generally speaking, the reason the church fails to have a more positive, transforming influence on our culture is that we do not fully grasp the Bible-based, Christ-centered, Spirit-empowered, God-glorifying perspective that belongs to us by grace—which is why we need to learn how to live the right worldview.

---

[20] Pat Morley documents these statistics in "The Case for a Men's Discipleship Program," *A Look in the Mirror* (no. 120), 1–2.

✚ 2

THE CENTER OF EVERYTHING

The purpose of this book is to help college students and others live wisely by thinking Christianly about daily life. To that end, we will trace the broad contours of the Christian worldview and sketch a few of its practical implications. To learn more about how the Christian worldview works itself out in various academic disciplines, the reader is encouraged to consult the other study guides published in this series. The present volume is written explicitly for Christians; however, it may also help non-Christians understand the way that Christians look at the world—not primarily by defending Christianity (which would require a much longer book) but simply by explaining it. One final qualification before we proceed: although the book's theology is largely shaped by the Protestant Reformation, much of what it says can also be affirmed by Christians from other traditions.

So far we have defined worldview as "a framework or set of fundamental beliefs through which we view the world and our calling and future in it."[1] Now we can begin to articulate the basic principles of any Christian worldview. In brief—and all of this will be explained in due course—such a worldview gives us four categories that theologians commonly use to understand human experience:

[1] James H. Olthuis, "On Worldviews," in Paul A. Marshall, Sander Griffioen, and Richard J. Mouw, eds., *Stained Glass: Worldviews and Social Science* (Lanham, MD: University Press of America, 1989), 29.

1) *Creation*: the way God created the world and everything in it, including the people he made in his own image, with the ultimate goal of displaying his glory;

2) *The Fall*: the way we turned away from our creator, choosing to live for ourselves rather than for our Father's glory, and thus came under the condemnation of a righteous God in a sin-cursed world;

3) *Grace*: the way God is working to save his people from sin and death through the crucifixion and resurrection of Jesus Christ, his Son, and then transforming our lives by the power of the Holy Spirit; and

4) *Glory*: the way God is fulfilling all his purposes for his people through the present and future preeminence of Jesus Christ over the everlasting kingdom of God.

Once we understand this four-part explanation of human experience—learning how to do what the poet T. S. Eliot called "thinking in Christian categories"[2]—we can apply it to every area of life. In doing so, we gain God's perspective on why any particular thing was made in the first place (*creation*), what has gone wrong with it (*the fall*), how we find its recovery in Jesus Christ (*grace*), and what it will become in the end, when everything is made new (*glory*).

These four stages of human history tell a complete and unified story that stretches back to before the very beginning and leans forward into eternity. God has always intended to make a beautiful place for the people he loves and to live with us there. I say "always," because the Bible describes eternal life as something that God "promised before the ages began and at the proper time manifested in his word" (Titus 1:2–3). Although that purpose seemingly has been frustrated by human sin, God is still working his plan—the eternal plan of redemption.

The story that the Bible tells about salvation is not simply one story among many stories or a tale that is part of some larger

---

[2] T. S. Eliot, *The Idea of a Christian Society* (New York: Harcourt, Brace, 1940), 26.

narrative. It is the story of all stories: the love story that begins and ends with the glory of God. It is also the story we live. We find our story within God's story and our narrative within his master narrative. In doing so, we find our purpose within his purpose and our mission in pursuing his mission.

THE GOD WHO IS THERE

Before we tell the story of the Christian worldview, we need to meet its Author. In doing so, we learn the answer to a couple of crucial questions that every worldview must answer: First, what is the fundamental reality? Second, how can we know that fundamental reality (or anything else, for that matter)? The place to begin answering these questions is where the Bible begins: "In the beginning, God . . ." (Gen. 1:1).

Every worldview has an integrating idea. The basic idea behind deism—which may be one of the most common worldviews in America today—is that a transcendent God made the universe but then more or less left it to run on its own. God is a creator but not a provider, and we are left to make our own way through life. Marxists and other materialists believe that there is no God at all, only the natural universe. People are merely bodies, not souls, so there is no transcendent basis for ethics. Buddhists believe that human beings must endure their earthly fate as they wait patiently to enter the state of nirvana. And so forth. These are only examples; readers will need to look elsewhere for a catalog of other worldviews or a full explanation of what they teach.[3] But suffice it to say that every worldview is animated by its central idea or driven by its main story line.

What unifies the Christian worldview, by contrast, is not merely an idea, but the being and character of Almighty God. The Bible does not present God as the conclusion to some logical

---

[3] James Sire provides a useful introduction to the main ideas of the most popular worldviews in *The Universe Next Door: A Basic Worldview Catalog*, 5th ed. (Downers Grove, IL: InterVarsity, 2009).

proof, or as a mystery beyond our comprehension, but treats his existence as the basic premise upon which everything else in the entire universe is built. God is always our ultimate frame of reference, the supreme reality at the center of all reality—the be-all and end-all of everything. Therefore, whatever else we include in our worldview will need to be understood with reference to God.

Christians believe that by denying the existence of God, atheism gets things wrong from the beginning. So does secular humanism, or any other worldview that puts the self at the center of the universe. We should not begin with ourselves at all, but with God, whose existence and nature are "the independent source and the transcendent standard for everything."[4] We start with God and work from there on up. Otherwise, the consequences are devastating, morally as well as intellectually. The Russian novelist Fyodor Dostoevsky was right when he said, "If God did not exist, everything would be permitted"[5]—including many things that are evil or cruel.

So we begin with the existence of God. However, mere belief in God is not enough. If there is a God, then we must believe in the God who is really there and not in some other deity. Most world religions believe in God (or gods, as the case may be), but their definition of deity may or may not stand within biblical boundaries. Furthermore, many people who say they are religious do not have a coherent definition of God at all, and thus their lives are prone to superstition. Or if they do have a clear definition of God, it springs more from their own desires than from divine revelation. According to the sociologist Christian Smith, today a majority of young Americans are adopting a "creed in which an undemanding God exists mostly to solve problems and make people feel good, a combination Divine Butler and Cosmic

---

[4] David K. Naugle, *Worldview: The History of a Concept* (Grand Rapids, MI: Eerdmans, 2002), 260.
[5] Fyodor Dostoevsky, *The Brothers Karamazov*, trans. Richard Pevear and Larissa Volokhonsky, Everyman's Library (New York: Alfred A. Knopf, 1990), 589.

Therapist, on call as needed."[6] Such a god is always available to meet needs and satisfy desires but never presumes to make demands or require sacrifices.

A notable example of a self-made deity for post-Christian times comes from an interview with the actor Chad Allen, who described how his own view of God reinforced his personal lifestyle:

> I judge all my actions by my relationship with god of my under-standing. It's very powerful, and it's taken its own shape and form. And I am very much at peace in the knowledge that in my heart God created this beautiful expression of my love. . . . It is a deep-founded, faith-based belief in god based upon the work that I've done growing up as a Catholic boy and then reaching out to Buddhist philosophy, to Hindu philosophy, to Native American beliefs and finally as I got through my course with addiction and alcoholism and finding a higher power that worked for me.[7]

By contrast, the Christian worldview does not begin with God as we would like him to be—the "god of my understanding." Instead, Christianity begins with the God who is really there. It's not about us; it's about him.

When we say "God," we mean the God of the Bible, in all his perfections, and not the god of the Koran, the Bhagavad Gita, or any other religious text. While other religions may portray certain aspects of his divine nature, only the Scriptures of the Old and New Testaments give us the full picture of God. The God of the Bible is all-knowing, all-present, all-powerful, and all-sufficient. He alone is infinite, eternal, and unchangeable in his wisdom, power, holi-ness, goodness, justice, truth, and love. He has revealed himself

---

[6] Christian Smith and Melinda Lundquist Denton, *Soul Searching: The Religious and Spiritual Lives of American Teenagers*, as quoted in Kevan Breitinger, "The kids have faith, so should the adults," *Philadelphia Inquirer* (March 12, 2005). See also Kenda Creasy Dean, *Almost Christian: What the Faith of Our Teenagers Is Telling the American Church* (New York: Oxford University Press, 2010).

[7] Chad Allen, in an interview televised on CNN's *Larry King Live!* (January, 2006).

as "The LORD, the LORD, a God merciful and gracious, slow to anger, and abounding in steadfast love and faithfulness, keeping steadfast love for thousands, forgiving iniquity and transgression and sin, but who will by no means clear the guilty" (Ex. 34:6–7). The biblical God is utterly and absolutely sovereign. He controls all things at all times and in all places, freely ordaining whatever comes to pass (Eph. 1:11). He is a God of pristine holiness, who punishes sin with righteous justice. He is also the God of crucified love, who has a plan for redeeming his people in Christ—the God who is "full of grace and truth" (John 1:14).

What else can we say about the one true God? He is "the King of the ages, immortal, invisible, the only God" (1 Tim. 1:17), who deserves all worship and eternal praise. He rules all nations and loves all the peoples of the earth. He is a deity of such powerful affection that nothing will ever be able to separate us from his love (Rom. 8:35–39). His highest end is the manifestation of his glory—the greatness and majesty of who he is, as revealed in what he does.

This one true and living God is triune. As the story of salvation unfolds, we discover that he is one God in three persons: the Father, the Son, and the Holy Spirit. Here we encounter a profound mystery, which distinguishes Christianity from other monotheistic worldviews such as Judaism and Islam. The Bible everywhere insists that there is one and only one God. Yet the Bible also reveals this God as a holy fellowship of three unique, distinct, and eternal persons. The true God is a tri-unity.

Even if the Christian doctrine of the Trinity can never be fully understood, it can be stated in seven simple propositions: (1) God the Father is God; (2) God the Son is God; (3) God the Holy Spirit is God; (4) the Father is not the Son; (5) the Son is not the Spirit; (6) the Spirit is not the Father; (7) nevertheless, there is only one God. These propositions may be illustrated in visual form (see Illustration 2.1).

Illustration 2.1

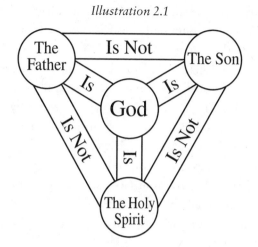

In his treatise *On Christian Doctrine*, the great North African theologian Augustine used somewhat different language to express the same eternal truths:

> The Father and the Son and the Holy Spirit, and each of these by Himself, is God, and at the same time they are all one God. The Father is not the Son nor the Holy Spirit; the Son is not the Father nor the Holy Spirit; the Holy Spirit is not the Father nor the Son: but the Father is only Father, the Son is only Son, and the Holy Spirit is only Holy Spirit.[8]

Although the doctrine of the Trinity can be stated in propositional form, the Trinity itself is no abstraction. On the contrary, the triune God is the lover at the heart of the universe. From everlasting to everlasting, there is one true God who exists as an intimate fellowship of three coequal and eternal persons—a God who finds infinite delight in the glory of his own being. The sovereign creator is also the eternal lover, who enjoys community as well as unity within the Godhead.

---

[8] Augustine, *Christian Doctrine*, Nicene and Post-Nicene Fathers, First Series, ed. Philip Schaff (1887; repr. Peabody, MA: Hendrickson, 1995), 1.5.

This triune God—the God of eternally loving relationships, who created us for community—is the one in whom we live and move and have our being (Acts 17:28). This is the God, said the apologist Francis Schaeffer, *who is there*.[9] And because he is there, he must be at the center of our worldview, as he is the center of everything else. The Christian worldview steadfastly maintains that God is the "ultimate reality whose trinitarian nature, personal character, moral excellence, wonderful works and sovereign rule constitute the objective reference point for all reality."[10] Nothing can be understood apart from God, writes John Piper, "and all understandings of all things that leave him out are superficial understandings, since they leave out the most important reality in the universe."[11]

HE IS NOT SILENT

The triune God of the Bible has spoken. As Francis Schaeffer went on to say, *He is there and he is not silent*.[12] God has revealed himself to us, so that we can know who he is. Just as importantly, he has revealed his purpose for us. If God had not spoken, how could we ever know the meaning of our existence? Because he has spoken to us, we have a vantage point that transcends our own perspective and enables us to see things as they truly are.

God has spoken to us both in the general revelation of creation and in the special revelation of his Word. The Protestant Reformers liked to say that God has given us two books. One book is creation; we know God by what he has made: "The heavens declare the glory of God, and the sky above proclaims his handiwork. Day to day pours out speech, and night to night reveals knowledge" (Ps. 19:1–2). "Every fact in nature is a revelation of God," wrote

---

[9] Francis A. Schaeffer, *The God Who Is There* (Downers Grove, IL: InterVarsity, 1968).

[10] Naugle, *Worldview,* 261.

[11] John Piper, *A God-Entranced Vision of All Things: The Legacy of Jonathan Edwards* (Wheaton, IL: Crossway, 2004), 24.

[12] Francis A. Schaeffer, *He Is There and He Is Not Silent* (Wheaton, IL: Tyndale, 1972).

the Scottish novelist and theologian George MacDonald, and each fact "is there such as it is because God is such as He is."[13] Even the bright blue flash of the kingfisher and the soaring flight of the eagle testify to the beauty and the majesty of God. Yet creation is not the only place where God has revealed himself. In order to help us know the way of salvation, he has also given us the book of his Word. As the psalmist went on to say: "The law of the LORD is perfect, reviving the soul; the testimony of the LORD is sure, making wise the simple" (Ps. 19:7). God is revealed in the words of Scripture as well as in the works of creation. The righteous law and saving gospel of the Old and New Testaments are part of his divine revelation—the true and trustworthy words of God. Galileo had both the Bible and the book of creation in view when he stated that "the Holy Scripture and nature derive equally from the godhead. . . . God reveals himself no less excellently in the effects of nature than in the sacred words of Scripture."[14]

The main theme of Scripture is the saving work of Jesus Christ, God the Son, who is the Word of God *incarnate* (John 20:31). This claim is unique to biblical Christianity. Christianity is the only religion or worldview to claim that God himself has become a man by taking on the flesh of humanity in the person of a single individual. Through the mystery of the virgin birth, at one and the same time Jesus of Nazareth is fully divine and fully human. This is essential to the whole story of salvation, as we shall see. For now, it is enough to say that God is revealed to us in the person of his Son. "In these last days," the Scripture says, God "has spoken to us by his Son" (Heb. 1:2). Indeed, to see the Son is to see the Father (John 6:46). Therefore, in Jesus Christ we have true knowledge of the living God.

It is only because God has revealed himself that it is possible

---

[13] George MacDonald, *Creation in Christ*, ed. Rolland Hein (Wheaton, IL: Harold Shaw, 1976), 145.
[14] Galileo Galilei, "Galileo's Letter to the Grand Duchess" (1615), in *The Galileo Affair: A Documentary History*, ed. Maurice A. Finocchiaro (Berkeley: University of California Press, 1989), 92–94.

for us to have a Christian view of the world. How can we know anything true about anything? Most importantly, how can we know the truth about our own purpose for life and place in the universe? We know these truths because God has revealed himself in what he does and what he says, in his works and in his Word, both written and incarnate. Furthermore, in coming to know Christ we gain access to an explicitly Christ-centered view of the world. He is the starting point for all of our thought. If we believe that Jesus Christ is the true Son of God—the one who *is* the truth (John 14:6)—then we will accept his view of God and of ourselves in sin and salvation.

Unless God had revealed himself to us, we would be limited to our own merely human perspectives. This is precisely what many non-Christians believe: that God has not spoken. The film critic Roger Ebert explained it like this: "Let me rule out at once any God who has personally spoken to anyone or issued any instructions to men. That some men believe they have been spoken to by God, I am certain. I do not believe Moses came down from the mountain with any tablets he did not go up with."[15] Some postmodern thinkers press their rejection of divine revelation to its logical extreme by denying that we have any transcendent perspective on reality at all. According to the philosopher Richard Rorty, there is "nothing deep down inside us except what we have put there ourselves," and "no standard of rationality . . . that is not obedient to our own conventions."[16] Truth itself is socially constructed. It is subjective, not objective, so all worldviews have an equal claim to the truth. There is no single, objective, overarching perspective that gives us a true and comprehensive explanation of the world. "Your worldview is just your opinion," people say. "You have your story, and I have my story, but there is no story that holds everything together."

---

[15] Roger Ebert, http://blogs.suntimes.com/ebert/2009/04/how_i_believe_in_g.html.
[16] Richard Rorty, quoted in Sire, *The Universe Next Door*, 228.

Christianity rejects such relativism because God has revealed himself, telling us one grand story of salvation and teaching us what is true, in distinction from what is false. Christianity is true to the way things are. It is "not a series of truths in the plural," said Francis Schaeffer, "but rather truth spelled with a capital 'T.' Truth about total reality, not just about religious things. Biblical Christianity is Truth concerning total reality—and the intellectual holding of that total Truth and then living in the light of that Truth."[17] Another way to say this is that the Christian faith is a unity of thought—truth that is interconnected. Christianity "is not just a lot of bits and pieces—there is a beginning and an end, a whole system of truth, and this system is the only system that will stand up to all the questions that are presented to us as we face the reality of existence."[18]

This does not mean, of course, that we have a perfect grasp of the truth or that we always do a very good job of living it out. We are culturally and historically situated, and thus we bear many of the limitations of our own time and place. Our finitude limits our knowledge, just as our fallenness distorts our understanding. This is as true for Christians as it is for anyone. We have only a partial grasp of the total truth.

God himself does not have the same limitation, however. He does not have a point of view; he has the complete view. And because he has revealed himself, we can see things from his vantage point—not perfectly yet truly. All truth is God's truth. That is to say, whatever things are true are things that God knows to be true, wherever we find them. Therefore, as Jonathan Edwards rightly said, all knowledge lies in the "agreement of our ideas with the ideas of God."[19] We are able to come to a true understanding of the

[17] Francis A. Schaeffer, quoted in Nancy Pearcey, *Total Truth: Liberating Christianity from Its Cultural Captivity* (Wheaton, IL: Crossway, 2004), 15.

[18] Schaeffer, *The God Who Is There*, in *The Complete Works of Francis Schaeffer: A Christian Worldview*, 5 vols. (Wheaton, IL: Crossway, 1982), 1:178.

[19] Jonathan Edwards, quoted in Duane Litfin, *Conceiving the Christian College* (Grand Rapids, MI: Eerdmans, 2004), 91.

world by thinking God's thoughts after him—however imperfectly or incompletely—and knowing the truth as he knows it to be.

"Once we grasp this principle"—namely, that all truth is God's truth, wherever it may be found—"then the worlds of literature, philosophy, history, science and art become the Christian's rightful domain."[20] Indeed, everything in the world becomes the Christian's rightful domain. Christianity is a God-given, Bible-based, Christ-centered worldview that gives us a coherent and comprehensive view of reality. This worldview begins with the infinite, personal, triune God who is there and is not silent, who was living in love before anyone or anything else ever existed. This loving God has revealed himself in the world that he made, in the inspired Word of the Bible, and in the incarnate Word of his Son. All meaning and purpose—including our own meaning and purpose—are defined in relationship to him. Thus the Christian worldview is not merely a set of propositions but a perspective on life that flows out of our friendship with a personal God, whose love writes our story.

---

[20] Arthur F. Holmes, *The Idea of a Christian College* (Grand Rapids, MI: Eerdmans, 1975), 25.

✚ 3

THE WAY WE WERE

We are part of one great story in which everything is moving toward the glory of God. Using a structure that goes as far back as Augustine in the fourth century, theologians commonly have told this story in four parts, as we noted earlier, organizing the Christian view of the world into four stages of redemptive history: creation, fall, grace, and glory.[1]

THE CREATOR/CREATURE DISTINCTION

The story opens with creation. Once again, we are simply following the logic of Scripture as it tells God's story: "In the beginning, God *created* the heavens and the earth" (Gen. 1:1). This is how the cosmos came into being. By his powerful word, God created the entire universe out of nothing (*ex nihilo*), "so that what is seen was not made out of things that are visible" (Heb. 11:3). He spoke the world into existence. The reason there is something rather than nothing—and the reason things are the way they are instead of the way they are not—is that God created them that way.

So there is a creator and there is a creation, and they are distinct. The creator is not to be confused with his creation, as if the universe itself were divine. This is the fundamental error of paganism and pantheism, which try to find deity somewhere within the material world. According to those worldviews, God *is* matter or is *in* matter—in human beings, perhaps, or in "Gaia," the goddess of the earth. But if the world itself has been created by a superior

---

[1] See Philip Graham Ryken, *Thomas Boston as Preacher of the Fourfold State*, Rutherford Studies in Historical Theology (Carlisle, UK: Paternoster, 1999), 57–85.

being, then our worship should not stop with the world or anything in it (which would be idolatry), but go beyond.

Nor is the material universe all there is, as if nature were the ultimate reality and matter the only thing that mattered. Rather than recognizing that the universe is governed by the providence of God—and understanding that whatever changes happen within the created order are part of his plan—materialism leaves everything to chance. Natural causes alone are sufficient to explain everything that exists. This naturalistic philosophy is summarized by Richard Dawkins, the well-known atheist and Oxford biologist who champions evolution as a godless worldview. Dawkins writes, "There is at bottom no design, no purpose, no evil, no good, nothing but blind, pitiless indifference."[2] This is the logical result of denying the existence of the creator. If the universe is what it is, without anyone behind it, then there is no ultimate purpose for anything, or any transcendent basis for making moral distinctions. Yet the truth is that the universe was designed by God for purposes that he intends. This creator/creature relationship is basic to Christianity as a worldview.

When we speak of God as the creator, we are once again speaking specifically of the triune God. Creation is not merely the work of the Father, but also of the Son and the Spirit. Right at the beginning of the Bible we read that as God fashioned the universe, "the Spirit of God was hovering over the face of the waters" (Gen. 1:2). The Bible also calls particular attention to the work of Christ as creator. "There is . . . one Lord, Jesus Christ," the Scripture says, "through whom are all things and through whom we exist" (1 Cor. 8:6). All things come from the Father, through the Son. "For by him"—that is, by Jesus Christ—"all things were created, in heaven and on earth, visible and invisible, whether thrones or dominions or rulers or authorities—all things were created through him and

[2] Richard Dawkins, *River out of Eden: A Darwinian View of Life* (New York: HarperCollins, 1995), 133.

for him" (Col. 1:16–17; cf. John 1:1–3). Because all things were created at his command, they are subject to his authority. Everything in creation relates to Jesus Christ, and nothing in the entire universe can be properly or completely understood apart from him.[3] John Piper celebrates this truth when he writes:

> All that came into being exists for Christ—that is, everything exists to display the greatness of Christ. Nothing—nothing!—in the universe exists for its own sake. Everything—from the bottom of the oceans to the top of the mountains, from the smallest particle to the biggest star, from the most boring school subject to the most fascinating science, from the ugliest cockroach to the most beautiful human—everything that exists, exists to make the greatness of Christ more fully known.[4]

If it is true that everything is from Christ and for Christ—and if it is true, further, that he holds everything together—then he is directly relevant to everything there is. This great truth makes Christianity a Christ-centered worldview from beginning to end. Jesus is not merely the agent of redemption, but also of creation. Jesus Christ is the Creator God. The universe was made by him, through him, and for him. Furthermore, at this very moment he is sustaining the whole creation by his providential care (Heb. 1:3). Whatever is happening in the world—down to the exact places where people live—is under his sovereign direction (Acts 17:24–27). Here is how Charles Colson summarizes the implications of creation and providence for human knowledge:

> In every topic we investigate, from ethics to economics to ecology, the truth is found only in relationship to God and his revelation. God created the natural world and natural laws. God created our bodies and the moral laws that keep us healthy. God

---

[3] Duane A. Litfin develops this theme at length in chapters 3 and 4 of *Conceiving the Christian College* (Grand Rapids, MI: Eerdmans, 2004). See also Mark A. Noll, *Jesus Christ and the Life of the Mind* (Grand Rapids, MI: Eerdmans, 2011).

[4] John Piper, *Spectacular Sins and Their Global Purpose in the Glory of Christ* (Wheaton, IL: Crossway, 2007), 33.

created our minds and the laws of logic and imagination. God created us as social beings and gave us the principles for social and political institutions. God created a world of beauty and the principles of aesthetics and artistic creation. In every area of life, genuine knowledge means discerning the laws and ordinances by which God has structured creation, and then allowing those laws to shape the way we should live.[5]

Creation and providence also have personal implications for our life in this world. Simply put, we owe our ongoing existence to Jesus Christ as the Son of God. The Protestant Reformer John Calvin found this great truth to be an occasion for worship and a basis for prayer. He wrote: "There cannot be found the least particle of wisdom, light, righteousness, power, rectitude or sincere truth which does not proceed from Him and claim Him for its author. . . . We should therefore learn to expect and supplicate all these things from Him, and thankfully acknowledge what He gives us."[6] Where the universe came from, where it is right now, and where it is going are all vitally connected to the person and work of Jesus Christ. Even the lilies of the field and the birds of the air are under his loving care (Matt. 6:26–30). "Wherever you cast your eyes," Calvin went on to say, "there is no spot in the universe wherein you cannot discern at least some sparks of his glory."[7]

KNOWING GOD, KNOWING OURSELVES

If the triune God is the creator, then creation shows us who God is. As we saw in the previous chapter, nature is one of the books that God has written to reveal his character. "What can be known about God is plain," wrote the apostle Paul, "because God has shown it. . . . His invisible attributes, namely, his eternal power and

[5] Charles Colson and Nancy Pearcey, *How Now Shall We Live?* (Wheaton, IL: Tyndale, 1999), 15.
[6] John Calvin, *Institutes of the Christian Religion*, ed. John T. McNeill; trans. Ford Lewis Battles; Library of Christian Classics, 20–21 (Philadelphia: Westminster, 1960), 1.5.1.
[7] Ibid.

divine nature, have been clearly perceived, ever since the creation of the world, in the things that have been made" (Rom. 1:19–20). Keen observers of nature recognize the handiwork of God and draw sound inferences about his attributes. "This most beautiful system of sun, planets, and comets," wrote Sir Isaac Newton, "could only proceed from the counsel and dominion of an intelligent and powerful Being."[8] Gerard Manley Hopkins made the same point more poetically: "The world is charged with the grandeur of God."[9]

At the same time that it teaches us who God is, creation also teaches us who *we* are. This is one of the fundamental questions any worldview has to answer: Who am I, and why am I here? In his poem "The Buried Life," Matthew Arnold writes about our wild, deep, and thirsty longing "to know whence our lives come and where they go."[10] Evolutionary naturalism—as distinct from a theistic worldview in which any changes we observe in the natural world are under the sovereign direction of God—says that we are merely the product of meaningless chance, and thus our lives do not have any given purpose or final destiny. Once we accept the theories of Charles Darwin, writes Christopher Manes, then we must "face the fact that the observation of nature has revealed not one scrap of evidence that humanity is superior or special, or even particularly more interesting than, say, lichen."[11] According to this culturally dominant creation story, the only purpose we have is whatever purpose we find for ourselves. "Gone is purpose," writes the Oxford chemist Peter Atkins. "Gone is the afterlife, gone is the soul, gone is protection through prayer, gone is design, gone is false comfort. All that is left is an exhilarating loneliness and the

---

[8] Isaac Newton, *Philosophiae Naturalis Principia Mathematica*, trans. Andrew Motte (New York: Daniel Adee, 1848), 504.

[9] Gerard Manley Hopkins, "God's Grandeur," in *Gerard Manley Hopkins: Poems and Prose* (New York: Penguin, 1985).

[10] Matthew Arnold, "The Buried Life," in *The Norton Anthology of English Literature*, rev. ed., ed. M. H. Abrams, 2 vols. (New York: Norton, 1968), 2:1021.

[11] Christopher Manes, *Green Rage: Radical Environmentalism and the Unmaking of Civilization* (Boston: Little, Brown, 1990), 142.

recognition that through science we can come to an understanding of ourselves and this glorious cosmos."[12]

Christianity responds by saying that our lives come from God. Thus our longing is satisfied in a person, or rather, three persons. The climax of creation came on the sixth day, when God said, "Let us make man" (Gen. 1:26). This divine declaration rules out the humanistic idea—first popularized by the ancient Greek philosopher Protagoras—that "man is the measure of all things." We did not make ourselves, and thus we cannot claim any right to define our identity. Who we are and what we are is ordained by God our maker. This truth is reinforced as the story of creation unfolds and God addresses the first man and the first woman directly, telling them to be fruitful and multiply, to subdue and rule the earth, and to eat from every tree except the Tree of the Knowledge of Good and Evil (Gen. 1:28–30; 2:16–17). We depend on God to speak to us and tell us the meaning and purpose of our existence.

The reason many people rebel against dependence on God is that they would prefer to determine their own destiny. Like the existentialist Jean-Paul Sartre, they claim, "There is no human nature, because there is no God to have a conception of it. . . . Man is nothing else but that which he makes of himself."[13] If what we are is not given to us by God, then we are free to live as we please, which is a dominating desire in Western culture, especially. The consequences of this worldview are lived out in broken lives and written into the art and literature of uncertainty and despair. By contrast, the Christian worldview maintains that human beings are not the random result of molecules in motion; we are the crown of creation, the highest product of creative design, the object of divine affection and intention. Although we come from the dust

---

[12] Peter W. Atkins, "Science and Religion: Rack or Featherbed: The Uncomfortable Supremacy of Science," *Science Progress* 83 (2000): 28–31.

[13] Jean-Paul Sartre, *Existentialism and Humanism*, in *The Modern Tradition: Backgrounds of Modern Literature*, ed. Richard Ellmann and Charles Fiedelson Jr. (New York: Oxford University Press, 1965), 828.

of the ground, God breathed life into us to make us living beings, body and soul (Gen. 2:7).

When God performed this creative act, he made us in his own image. This high privilege must be of crucial importance because it is mentioned three times in the space of two verses: "Then God said, 'Let us make man in our image, after our likeness. . . .' So God created man in his own image, in the image of God he created him; male and female he created them" (Gen. 1:26–27). Like a newly minted coin, an image is something fashioned according to the pattern of an original. Therefore, for women and men to be made in the divine image is for us to be made like God—in such aspects of our personhood as rationality, spirituality, creativity, community, morality, and authority.[14] What constitutes the unique sanctity of all human life—from conception to the grave, and beyond—is that God has made us like himself. This is the biblical view of the human person.

The divine image gives us an important clue about what human beings are made for. If who we are is a reflection of who God is, then we do not exist by ourselves or for ourselves but in relationship to God. God has made us like himself so that we can hear him, know him, love him, worship him, and serve him. The Westminster Shorter Catechism famously summarizes our purpose in relationship to God by saying that humanity's "chief end is to glorify God and enjoy him forever." God's primary goal is his glory, as the Father, the Son, and the Holy Spirit each try to honor one another. Within their eternal fellowship, the three persons of the Trinity are not self-seeking but self-giving. This is also God's intention for us. We are not designed or destined for our purposes but for his. We are made to display God's triune majesty, and we have no purpose or significance apart from him. Our highest joy and true reason for being is to take pleasure in the infinite beauty

---

[14] For a complete biblical analysis of the image of God in people, see Philip Edgcumbe Hughes, *The True Image: The Origin and Destiny of Man in Christ* (Leicester: Inter-Varsity, 1989).

of God. So the psalmist teaches us to say, "Not to us, O LORD, not to us, but to your name give glory" (Ps. 115:1).

HOW TO GLORIFY GOD

There is a creator, and there are creatures made in his image who are called to glorify him—that is, to give him all of the worship and honor that someone with his supreme majesty deserves.

The place where we glorify our maker is within his good creation. Here we remember the value judgment that our creator placed on everything he made. After each day of creation, God looked at what he had made and saw that it was good. And when he was finished, "God saw everything that he had made, and behold, it was *very* good" (Gen. 1:31). Over against the dualistic worldview of Islam, for example, which maintains that good and evil are equally ultimate, the Bible says that what God made in the beginning was perfectly good. This divine approbation gives us the Christian view of creation: it was all made good for the glory of God, with the further implication that there should be no separation between the sacred and the secular. If God created everything good, then his people cannot restrict their faith to private religion but must pursue his purposes in every sphere of life, whether public or private. Christianity is a world-affirming worldview that embraces the entire creation as a gift from God.

Admittedly, some Christians have always been suspicious of at least some aspects of creation. When it comes to physical pleasures such as good food and fine drink, they often abstain, but when they indulge, they do it with the suspicion of a guilty conscience. The apostle Paul rejected this sub-Christian worldview by celebrating the bounty of creation: "Everything created by God is good, and nothing is to be rejected if it is received with thanksgiving" (1 Tim. 4:4); "so, whether you eat or drink, or whatever you do, do all to the glory of God" (1 Cor. 10:31). This does not mean that the good things of God's creation are not subject to sinful

abuse, as we shall see. But the good things we do in the body—
even basic things such as eating and drinking—are under the blessing of our Creator God. The body is not an impediment to the
soul but an instrument for glorifying God.

Here we can make some direct connections to daily life. Our
real worldview is not merely the one we say we believe but the one
we actually live in the world. It is not an intellectual construct but
a set of practices. So how do we live out the Christian doctrine of
creation?

We start from the premise that God made us to glorify him in
his good creation. *The Children's Catechism* expresses this truth
with beautiful simplicity:

1) Who made you? *God.*
2) What else did God make? *God made all things.*
3) Why did God make you and all things? *For his own glory.*

These questions are simple enough for even the smallest child to
learn, and yet anyone who knows the answers is well on the way
to knowing the Christian worldview. All we need to do now is
to extend the goal of glorifying God to every aspect of life. We
fully understand the purpose of anything we do to the extent that
we understand the particular way that it brings praise to God.
Whatever we are doing—whether we are playing baseball, shovel-
ing snow, or choosing artwork to hang on the wall—we ought to
be able to say (and know why we say it), "This is for you, Lord. It
is all for your glory."

In what ways can we give glory to God? Most obviously,
perhaps, we glorify God with our praise, worshiping the creator
rather than anything in his good creation. It is not enough for us
simply to acknowledge God's bare existence; we must celebrate his
majesty by singing and speaking the honor of his name. "God is
glorified," said Jonathan Edwards, "not only by His glory's being

seen, but by its being rejoiced in."[15] This is where we will find our highest joy and greatest satisfaction: in the worship of our Creator God. Augustine famously said, "You stir man to take pleasure in praising you, because you have made us for yourself, and our heart is restless until it rests in you."[16] We are made for praise, as Augustine understood. Everyone finds someone or something to worship. But the only object of worship that brings true satisfaction to the soul is the one true God.

We are also called to glorify God with our bodies. The doctrine of creation affirms the goodness of the human body as designed and manufactured by God. The body is not the source of sinful corruption; nor is it a prison that the soul needs to escape. Rather, the body is part of God's good creation, and therefore it can be used for his glory. Our eyes and ears, hands and feet, and mouths and brains are all instruments for serving God.

The inherent goodness of our bodies includes our sexuality. God has made us as sexual beings, male and female, and this too is part of the creation that God called "good." The Christian worldview celebrates sexual intercourse as a gift to be received in marriage with gratitude, reverence, and joy. When God told Adam and Eve to be fruitful and multiply (Gen. 1:28), it was his design for this mandate to be fulfilled exclusively through marital relations. The sexual intimacy that Adam and Eve shared was the seal of their covenant relationship, expressing their total spiritual union in covenant before God. Their sons and daughters would spring from the joy of their one-flesh union.

The doctrine of creation thus affirms marriage—and beyond marriage, the family—as the basic love relationship and building block of human society. It further specifies that marriage consists of one man united to one woman in a love covenant for life (a specification that morally excludes any sexual union outside the sacred

---

[15] Jonathan Edwards, "Miscellanies," no. 448, in *The Works of Jonathan Edwards*, ed. Thomas Schafer (New Haven, CT: Yale University Press, 1994), 13:495.

[16] Augustine, *Confessions*, trans. Henry Chadwick (Oxford: Oxford University Press, 1991), 1.1.

vows of marriage). The biblical ethic for sexuality does not come from some arbitrary decree (still less from human invention), but from the very structure of creation itself.

So does the Bible's call to community. God told Adam that it was not good for him to be alone (Gen. 2:18). This was the only thing in all creation that God said was not good: Adam's loneliness. As a human being he was a social being, made to live in community, sharing life in interdependent relationships with other people made in the image of God. From the beginning, God gave him a woman to be his partner, and in time their loving relationship would grow into a family, a community, a city. This was God's design, and as a result, creation carried within it the potentiality of culture.

This does not mean, of course, that God calls everyone to be married. Marriage is part of God's good creation—a divinely ordained institution that is crucial to God's purposes for humanity and a primary place for husbands and wives, fathers and mothers, to live for the glory of God. Yet singleness is a prime opportunity to live with single-hearted devotion to Christ, as the Bible emphasizes (1 Cor. 7:7–8, 32–35), and also as Jesus exemplified: in his earthly life, the Son of God remained single. Furthermore, our relationships as brothers and sisters in Christ give us all a place to belong. The church is not simply *like* a family. On the contrary, our family relationships in the body of Christ take precedence over our nuclear or biological family (Matt. 12:46–50). When God provided Eve for Adam, he was doing something more than establishing marriage: he was drawing all of his people into community.

We are also called to glorify God in our work. Work itself is not a result of humanity's fall into sin but a good gift from God, given with creation. In the beginning work was not a curse, as some have believed, but a calling. God put Adam in the garden "to work it and keep it" (Gen. 2:15)—in other words, to take care of it. Then he gave Eve to serve as Adam's helper in doing this good work, so that together as equal partners they could fulfill God's calling. Just as God had done the work of creation (Gen. 2:2), so too he gave work to his people, as a gift. As Adam said to Eve in John Milton's epic poem, *Paradise Lost*:

> Man hath his daily work of body or mind
> Appointed, which declares his dignity,
> And the regard of Heaven on all his ways.[17]

Whatever God has called us to do in our daily employment—whatever goods we produce and services we provide—is honorable because we are made in the image of a working God. Whether we are students or teachers or bankers or dancers, the Bible says, "There is nothing better for a person than that he should eat and drink and find enjoyment in his toil" (Eccles. 2:24).

We are called to glorify God in our rest as well as in our work. This too is part of the created order. God did the work of creation in six days but rested on the seventh day (Gen. 2:2). Then, in his goodness, he gave us the benefit of imitating him by resting from our work one full day out of seven. God designed us to follow his pattern of labor and leisure (Gen. 2:3). The Sunday rest that comes through worship and God-centered recreation is part of what it means to be created in his image. But even beyond the divine gift of this weekly pattern, there are opportunities for leisure as well as labor in the rhythms of our daily routine. Many Christians leave too little time for play or else treat what ought to be play as another form of work. But hiking through the woods, playing tag with children, sailing a boat, knitting a scarf, and enjoying other body-renewing, soul-restoring forms of recreation give us opportunities to rest in God and enjoy the goodness of his gifts.

---

[17] John Milton, *Paradise Lost* (New York: Holt, Rinehart & Winston, 1951), book 4, lines 618–20.

THE CREATION MANDATE

How else can we glorify God? The doctrine of creation affirms the environment, where we have a responsibility of benevolent stewardship. God said, "Be fruitful and multiply and fill the earth and subdue it, and have dominion over the fish of the sea and over the birds of the heavens and over every living thing that moves on the earth" (Gen. 1:28). This command is part of what theologians call "the creation mandate," or "cultural mandate." Human beings have been designated to represent God's rule on earth. God has placed the wealth of his creation under our oversight (Ps. 8:5–8). Everything still belongs to him, of course, for "to the LORD your God belong heaven and the heaven of heavens, the earth with all that is in it" (Deut. 10:14). Nevertheless, God has placed what he owns into our protective care. God planted a garden, but then he put people in that garden "to work it and take care of it" (Gen. 2:15 NIV). We have the privilege of stewardship without the prerogatives of ownership. This calling gives us the right to use the resources of creation for the good of humanity and the glory of God but not to abuse our environment in ways that harm God's creatures or hinder human flourishing for generations to come.[18]

More positively, the creation mandate invites us to revel in the beauty and wonder of everything that God has made, from the scarlet sunset that glimmers in the Western sky to the craggy peak of a distant mountain. The world we live in is to be neither deified nor exploited but nurtured and enjoyed. Calvin presented a complete Christian perspective on creation care when he wrote:

> The custody of the garden was given in charge to Adam, to show that we possess the things which God has committed to our hands, on the condition that, being content with a frugal and moderate use of them, we should take care of what shall

---

[18] Fred Van Dyke gives a thorough summary of Christian thinking about creation care in *Between Heaven and Earth: Christian Perspectives on Environmental Protection* (Westport, CT: Praeger, 2010).

remain. Let him who possesses a field, so partake of its yearly fruits, that he may not suffer the ground to be injured by his negligence: but let him endeavor to hand it down to posterity as he received it, or even better cultivated. Let him so feed on its fruits, that he neither dissipates it by luxury, nor permits it to be marred or ruined by neglect. Moreover, that this economy, and this diligence, with respect to those good things that God has given us to enjoy, may flourish among us; let everyone regard himself as the steward of God in all things which he possesses.[19]

At the same time that the doctrine of creation calls us to enjoy nature, it also gives us a basis for investigating the natural world through science. Far from conflicting with science, creation makes science possible by establishing an orderly universe in which sense perception gives us trustworthy information about what is really there. Here is how one contemporary thinker explains the theological basis for science:

The universality of objective intelligibility (assumed by any honest scientist) can be explained only through recourse to a transcendent subjective intelligence that has thought the world into being, so that every act of knowing a worldly object or event is literally a recognition, a thinking again of what has already been thought by a primordial divine power.[20]

Already in the garden of Eden, Adam began the scientific work of classification as he gave each animal its proper name (Gen. 2:19–20). The people of God have been keenly interested in the study of science ever since, partly as a way to explore the mind of our maker. Properly understood, science is not merely the study of the physical universe but also an exploration of what God has made. According to the second article of the Belgic Confession, which was first published in 1561, "The universe is before our eyes like a

---

[19] John Calvin, *Commentaries on the First Book of Moses Called Genesis* (Grand Rapids, MI: Eerdmans, 1948), 125.
[20] Robert Barron, *The Priority of Christ: Toward a Postliberal Catholicism* (Grand Rapids, MI: Brazos, 2007), 154.

beautiful book in which all creatures, great and small, are as letters to make us ponder the invisible things of God." As the famous
astronomer Johannes Kepler surveyed the heavens, with all their
mathematical precision, and as he pondered the "invisible things
of God," he believed that in effect he was thinking God's thoughts
after him. Kepler wrote, "God, who founded everything in the
world according to the norm of quantity, also has endowed man
with a mind which can comprehend these norms." Furthermore,
"God wanted us to recognize them by creating us after his image
so that we could share in his own thoughts."[21] Science is a gift from
God that gives us as much opportunity as theology does to know
the mind of our maker. Although the Creator God is infinitely separate from his creation, wrote Cardinal John Henry Newman, "yet
He has so implicated Himself with it and taken it into His very
bosom by His presence in it, His providence over it, His impres-
sions upon it, and His influences through it, that we cannot truly
or fully contemplate it without contemplating Him."[22]

The doctrine of creation also affirms music and the arts. While
there is nothing specific about this in Genesis 1 and 2, by Genesis 4
we are introduced to Jubal as "the father of all those who play the
lyre and pipe" (v. 21). What we do with sound and sight is part of
the inherent potentiality of creation. This is dynamically displayed
in the vast diversity of music and art produced by every people
group and every culture in the world. Whether they intend to do so
or not, artists and musicians who portray the good, the true, and
the beautiful are fulfilling a divine calling to creativity. According
to artist Makoto Fujimura, "All artists, regardless of their faith,
are breathing Eden's air when they create."[23] Nonartists do some-

[21] Johannes Kepler, letters to Herwart von Hohenburg, as quoted in Gerald Holton, *Thematic Origins of Scientific Thought* (Cambridge, MA: Harvard University Press, 1973), 84; and A. C. Crombie, *Augustine to Galileo*, 2nd ed., 2 vols. (Cambridge, MA: Harvard University Press, 1961), 2:195.
[22] John Henry Newman, *The Idea of a University*, ed. Frank M. Turner (New Haven, CT: Yale University Press, 1996), 37.
[23] Makoto Fujimura, "Breathing Eden's Air," *Books and Culture* (July/August, 2012): 9.

thing similar when they move to the rhythm of good music or receive visual art as a gift. Our creator tells us, "Whatever is true, whatever is honorable, whatever is just, whatever is pure, whatever is lovely, whatever is commendable, if there is any excellence, if there is anything worthy of praise, think about these things" (Phil. 4:8). But do not just think about such things: talk about them, write about them, sing about them, paint them, dramatize them, film them, and explore their truth and beauty in all the arts.

Marriage and family. Work and leisure. Science and creation care. Music and the arts. Together these varied aspects of human life comprise our cultural mandate. Based on the command to fill, subdue, and rule the earth (Gen. 1:28), we have a God-given responsibility to develop the possibilities of creation in ways that reveal our maker's praise, and ultimately fill the whole earth with his glory (Hab. 2:14). It is not just one part of life that ought to glorify God, but all of life, in all its fullness. This is the way things were meant to be.

4

PARADISE LOST

Sadly, the way things were meant to be is not the way things are. Something has gone badly wrong, and it went wrong almost from the beginning. As fundamental as creation is to the Christian worldview, the Bible spends surprisingly little time reporting how it happened—mainly a couple of pages in Genesis. Presumably, this is because humanity fell so quickly and suddenly into sin.

IN THE GARDEN

To understand how humanity sinned, we need to know the law that God required Adam to keep. To glorify God completely is to love him wholeheartedly, trust him unreservedly, and obey him absolutely. In the words of Michel de Montaigne, the famous French essayist, "To obey is the proper office of a rational soul."[1] God is to be obeyed simply because he is God. To prove their obedience God gave our first parents a clear and simple prohibition: "You are free to eat from any tree in the garden; but you must not eat from the Tree of the Knowledge of Good and Evil, for when you eat from it you will certainly die" (Gen. 2:16–17 NIV). With these words, God spoke Adam into the personhood of moral agency. In effect, he also established a covenant with Adam. It was a covenant of creation, in which the first man—representing all humanity— was duty bound to perfect obedience. God made a moral universe in which the reward for obeying him was life, but the punishment for disobeying him was death.

---

[1] Michel de Montaigne, *Essays of Montaigne*, vol. 5, trans. Charles Cotton, rev. William Carew Hazlett (New York: Edwin C. Hill, 1910), 28.

The Tree of the Knowledge of Good and Evil was the ideal test of man's fidelity. The only thing it demanded was the only thing that mattered: pure and loving obedience to the revealed will of God. Knowing that this particular tree was forbidden was not something that could be read off creation; it could only be revealed by God. So Adam had to choose whether to live for God or for himself. In making this choice he was—as the Puritans sometimes put it—"able to stand, but free to fall." If he made the right choice, he would live forever, fulfilling the creation mandate, filling and subduing the earth with the help of godly offspring, and developing the full potential of human civilization in covenant with God.

That is not what happened, however. Our first parents had everything to lose by tasting the forbidden fruit and nothing to gain worth gaining. Nevertheless, they sought their own independence and broke covenant with God: "The woman . . . took of its fruit and ate, and she also gave some to her husband, who was with her, and he ate" (Gen. 3:6). In these few words are contained the sum of human misery. Until this moment, human beings had known only the good. Now they also knew evil, to their dismay and destruction.

Here it is crucial to understand that the fall was a real event that took place in space-time history. There was a man, Adam, who took a piece of fruit from a woman, Eve, put it in his mouth, and swallowed it. This is not merely allegory; it is history. Christianity identifies the beginning of evil in the world by showing its human origin in a genuinely historical event. There is a sense in which this history gets repeated every time that anyone makes a sinful choice. But because of his divinely ordained role as our moral representative, the first sin of the first Adam is foundational for all that follows.

TRAGIC CONSEQUENCES

From that point on, everything has gone badly wrong. So let us lament the many tragic consequences of sin, starting with guilt.

Even before they could wipe the juice off their chins, Adam and Eve knew that they were sinners: "The eyes of both of them were opened, and they realized they were naked" (Gen. 3:7 NIV). Their unprecedented shame over their nakedness was a telltale sign of their guilt before God. And because of our solidarity with Adam as our covenant representative, the juice of his first sin ran down our chins as well. This is part of the profound unity of the human race. Not only are we all "made from one man" (Acts 17:26), but all of us have also sinned in one man. "Sin came into the world through one man," the Scripture says; "one trespass led to condemnation for all men" (Rom. 5:12, 18). According to the doctrine of original sin, the entire human race was condemned in Adam and has received from him a sinful nature. "Certainly nothing jolts us more rudely than this doctrine," wrote Blaise Pascal, the famous French philosopher, "and yet, but for this mystery the most incomprehensible of all, we remain incomprehensible to ourselves."[2] We are all guilty from birth and therefore born under divine judgment. Adam's fall was our fall, the fall of humanity into sin, which we are only too willing to ratify by our own guilty sins.

Sin also brings alienation. Formerly Adam and Eve had walked with God in the cool of the day. They did this because they loved God and wanted to be with him. But now "they hid themselves from the presence of the LORD God among the trees of the garden" (Gen. 3:8). Sinners know instinctively that God is too holy to look upon their sin. This explains why our first parents dreaded the sound of the divine footfall in Eden. When they heard God coming, they literally hid "from his face." This is what we all do. We hide from God, not wanting to confess our sin against him or acknowledge his claim upon our lives (Col. 1:21) yet all the while still desperate to find him. We were made to love and enjoy God, and we will never find true and lasting satisfaction apart from a relationship with him. But sin brings separation, which leads us to start looking for satisfaction

---

[2] Blaise Pascal, *Pensées*, 65.

in all the wrong places. Rather than taking true delight in God and moving at every moment toward him, there are many times when we want nothing to do with God at all—when we are not hungry to hear his Word or happy to sing his praises.

The loneliness that sin brings is horizontal as well as vertical, affecting not only our relationship with God (the vertical), but also our relationships with other people (the horizontal). Having rebelled against God, we now find ourselves estranged from one another. Sometimes the problem is that we expect too much from other people. Longing for relationship, we hope that friends, lovers, and family members can give us something that it turns out only God himself can provide. Our desire for relationships is good, but we demand too much, and soon our disappointment with other people turns to conflict.

The breach between Adam and Eve became obvious the moment they sinned and felt the need to protect themselves from the unbearable scrutiny of another human being by wearing clothes. Soon Adam launched his first assault on his estranged wife. When God asked if he had eaten the forbidden fruit, Adam said, "The woman you put here with me—*she* gave me some fruit from the tree, and I ate it" (Gen. 3:12 NIV). This was hardly chivalrous. Adam's confession ("and I ate it") seems to come as an afterthought. His real concern was to shift the blame to Eve (not to mention God), and this is the way of fallen human beings ever since: we excuse our sin by saying it was someone else's fault.

We can only imagine the bitter arguments that Adam and Eve had during the long, sad years after Eden. "If only you had never eaten that forbidden fruit!" Eve would say. "Well, you ate it first!" Adam would retort. In *Paradise Lost*, John Milton describes their endless recriminations: "Thus they in mutual accusation spent / The fruitless hours, but neither self condemning; / And of their vain contest appeared no end."[3] Milton was right—there is no

---

[3] John Milton, *Paradise Lost* (New York: Holt, Rinehart & Winston, 1951), book 9, lines 1187–89.

end to human conflict. Always sinned against but never sinning, everyone a victim but never a villain, there is discord and disharmony at every level of human relationships.

Estrangement is common in the home, where husbands are angry or unfaithful, wives are critical or judgmental, and far too many marriages end in divorce. Children disobey their parents, while parents exasperate their children. The elderly are killed in the name of mercy, while the unborn never see the light of day. There is also estrangement in the church, where each group claims to have God on its side and looks down on people who do not think, or worship, or serve the way they do.

Then there is estrangement in society, where men and women wage an endless battle of the sexes, often to the disadvantage or exploitation of women. There is estrangement in the workplace, where competitors use and abuse one another to get ahead in their careers, and where corporate greed claims excessive profits off the backs of ordinary employees and out of the pocketbooks of helpless investors. Bosses abuse their power and workers rise up in rebellion. We see the same thing in the wider economy, where exploitation is so woven into the fabric of the global marketplace that the poor are often enmeshed in the cords of injustice. And there is estrangement around the globe, especially in the form of armed conflict. Nation rises against nation, and tribe against tribe; dictators oppress their own people; terrorists commit random acts of violence; and superpowers provide weapons that fuel the fires of war. We are not guided by love but held captive to hatred.

TOTAL DEPRAVITY

Christianity offers the most accurate explanation for all of these broken relationships by calling sin a sin. How depraved our desires have become, and how far we have fallen from the beautiful image of God! This is the tragedy of the human condition: "All have sinned and fall short of the glory of God" (Rom. 3:23).

If creation is normal, then the fall has made us abnormal. Traces of our original goodness still remain, to be sure, but now we are horribly corrupted by sin. As Pascal observed, there is within us both "some great principle of greatness and some great principle of wretchedness."[4] C. S. Lewis expresses the same truths more poetically in one of his Chronicles of Narnia, where the lion-king Aslan says to human beings, "You come of the Lord Adam and the Lady Eve. And that is both honor enough to erect the head of the poorest beggar, and shame enough to bow the shoulders of the greatest emperor on earth."[5]

To change the metaphor, God's reflection in us has become distorted like a face in a carnival mirror. Such is our depravity that every part of every person is warped by sin. Sin corrupts our hearts so that we set our affections on unholy desires. It corrupts our feelings so that we are in emotional turmoil. It corrupts our wills so that we will not choose the good. Our whole nature is corrupted by sin. This is what theologians mean when they speak of "total depravity"—not that we are as sinful as we could possibly be, but that we are sinners through and through.

Sin divides our hearts and distorts our desires so that we do not love what God invites us to love. Every sin flows from some failure in our affections. Sin also corrupts our minds so that now we are unable to think God's thoughts after him. We misunderstand, misconstrue, misinterpret, and misvalue. In our fallen nature, we are not able to comprehend the Christian worldview, let alone live by its principles. Paul said it like this: "The natural person does not accept the things of the Spirit of God, for they are folly to him, and he is not able to understand them because they are spiritually discerned" (1 Cor. 2:14). Because of the mind's influence on the rest of a person's life, the tragic results are pervasive. As the fourth-century theologian Athanasius wrote in his famous treatise

---

[4] Pascal, *Pensées*, 149.
[5] C. S. Lewis, *Prince Caspian* (London: William Collins, 1981), 191.

On the Incarnation, fallen human beings "did not raise their gaze to the truth, but sated themselves even more with evils and sins, so that they no longer appeared rational, but from their ways of life were reckoned irrational."[6]

In describing the noetic effects of sin—the intellectual impact of our fallen nature—the Bible often uses images of darkness and blindness: "They are darkened in their understanding, alienated from the life of God because of the ignorance that is in them, due to their hardness of heart" (Eph. 4:18); and "The god of this world has blinded the minds of the unbelievers, to keep them from seeing the light of the gospel of the glory of Christ" (2 Cor. 4:4). Even what the book of nature tells us about the character of God is closed to us because of our sin (Rom. 1:18–21). As a result of the blindness that sin induces, the reasons that people have for rejecting the Christian worldview are not merely rational; they are also spiritual. Nor are people who embrace a Christian worldview entirely immune to the intellectual effects of sin. Our thinking, too, is damaged by our depravity, even when it comes to our interpretation of Scripture.

We see the effects of our sin in every area of life—the same areas of life, in fact, that we considered earlier as part of God's creative intention for humanity. We do not honor the God who is there in our worship or give him thanks for his good creation. Instead, we seek our own glory. Rather than worshiping the creator, we worship things that he has created: "For although they knew God, they did not honor him as God or give thanks to him, but they became futile in their thinking, and their foolish hearts were darkened. . . . They exchanged the truth about God for a lie and worshiped and served the creature rather than the Creator" (Rom. 1:21, 25). Usually these verses are taken to refer to idolatry as it was practiced in the ancient world, with objects of silver

---

[6] Athanasius, *On the Incarnation*, trans. John Behr (Yonkers, NY: St. Vladimir's Seminary Press, 2011), 62.

and stone. Yet people continue to worship created things today—everything from the designer labels that drive the fashion industry to the obsessive attachment that some fans have to their favorite sports teams. "What each one honors before all else," wrote Origen the theologian sometime during the third century, "what before all things he admires and loves, this for him is God."

Due to the corruption of our sin, we often fail to glorify God with our physical bodies. In fact, the very parts of our bodies become instruments of unrighteousness. Nowhere is this more true than in our sexuality. Consider all the lust, self-gratification, perversion, and abuse involved in sexual sin, and then consider all the damage that is done in our lives when sexuality is used in ways contrary to God's good design. Sexual intercourse is the covenant cement that is designed to unite one man and one woman for life. But when sex is shared with the wrong person, at the wrong time, or for the wrong purpose, the wrong things get attached. After the bodies uncouple, souls are torn apart, and the best and deepest intimacy is squandered. Although sexual promiscuity sometimes brings disease, the real danger is to relationships, including our relationship with God himself. Even the way we talk about sex—as something to "have" rather than to "give"—reveals the brokenness of this aspect of life.

Another place where we fail to glorify God is in the work of our calling. According to the curse of the fall—God's righteous judgment against Adam's sin (Gen. 3:17–18)—humanity still has to subdue the earth, but now labor has become a labor. The ground will only yield its fruit at the cost of sweaty toil, for the creation itself is frustrated by sin (Rom. 8:20). Now, instead of simply tending a garden, the man has to turn the wilderness *into* a garden. This curse of thorn and thistle is not just for farmers; it is for everyone who lives east of Eden. The factory, the boardroom, and the cubicle have become places of corruption and oppression, and we all experience the drudgery and dissatisfaction that so often come with working on the job. Like Solomon, the biblical philosopher, we sigh, "What does a man get for all the toil and anxious striving with which he labors?" (Eccles. 2:22 NIV).

The curse of the fall extends to the family, where husbands and wives fight to gain the upper hand (Gen. 3:19), and where the woman is afflicted in her unique calling as wife and mother (Gen. 3:16). Men also suffer in their unique calling as husbands and fathers, of course, but God announces a curse to Eve—a curse that refers to the physical pains of childbirth and to much more besides. It refers to childbearing in general and thus to all the frustrations associated with motherhood in a fallen world, including not getting married, not having children, and the heartaches of raising and sometimes losing children. Taken together, the curses that men and women must endure mean that the two most basic tasks of any generation—namely, making a living and raising children—are only fulfilled through suffering.

We also see the effects of sin in our neglect of the environment. Given what the Bible says about how God is revealed in his creation, such neglect is virtually a blasphemy. Rather than sharing what God has given to us and using it for his redemptive project, we squander his resources by using them for our own purposes and pleasures. We abuse creation by making bad use of good things.[7] The consequences of these sins, which may linger for generations, go far beyond the human race to affect the world around us. Creation retains "vestiges of the glory of God that shine through the corruption of the universe blighted by sin."[8] Nevertheless, the creation groans under the weight of human sin, suffering futility until it is released from its bondage by the second coming of the Son of God (Rom. 8:19–22).

We see the further effects of sin whenever science and

---

[7] See St. Cyril, *The Catechetical Lectures*, trans. Edwin H. Gifford, *Nicene and Post-Nicene Fathers*, vol. 7, ed. Philip Schaff and Henry Ware (Peabody, MA: Hendrickson, 1994), 49.

[8] R. Albert Mohler Jr., "A God-Centered Worldview," in *For the Fame of God's Name: Essays in Honor of John Piper*, ed. Sam Storms and Justin Taylor (Wheaton, IL: Crossway, 2010), 361.

technology are developed in destructive ways that lead to death instead of life (such as coming up with deadlier weapons), or in dehumanizing ways that treat people more like machines than like persons (such as the harvesting of human embryos for scientific research). The Dutch theologian Abraham Kuyper summarizes the problem well: "Sin is what lures and tempts people to place science outside of a relationship with God, thereby stealing science from God, and ultimately turning science against God."[9] To give one notable example, when the first computer flickered to life in 1950—the machine called MANIAC—its first job was to carry out the calculations necessary to build the hydrogen bomb. Considering the bomb's exponential increase in deadly force led one historian to conclude that the computer was "conceived in sin."[10]

We also see the effects of sin in music and the arts, where today a tragic loss of sacred beauty produces absurdity, irrationality, and even cruelty. The problem here is not with artists being honest about the human condition, which is part of telling the truth. Artists with integrity necessarily wrestle with the ugly and uncomfortable implications of our sinful condition.[11] The problem is with artists who glory in depravity. We even see the corruption of sin in our play. Think of all the cheating in amateur and professional sports through the use of performance-enhancing drugs—the corruption of competition. Or else consider the way that Americans labor at their leisure, devoting as much energy and expense into entertaining themselves as they put into engaging in productive work that benefits other people.

These examples show the suffering that sin has brought into the world. They also display the clarity that the doctrine of the fall brings to all our suffering. Now we can see why things have

[9] Abraham Kuyper, *Wisdom and Wonder: Common Grace in Science and Art*, ed. Jordan J. Ballor and Stephen J. Grabill, trans. Nelson D. Kloosterman (Grand Rapids, MI: Christian's Library Press, 2011), 51.

[10] Jim Holt, "How the Computers Exploded," *New York Review of Books* (June 7, 2012), 32.

[11] See Theodore L. Prescott, ed., *A Broken Beauty* (Grand Rapids, MI: Eerdmans, 2005).

gone so badly wrong. Every serious worldview admits that there is something wrong, attempts a diagnosis, and prescribes a cure. But Christianity explains the misery and apparent meaninglessness of our existence better than anything else. The reason we do all the wrong things we do is that we do not have a right relationship with God. This explains why people hold back from making commitments and then break the commitments they make. It explains the power of our addictions and the pervasiveness of cheating in academia. It explains why the average worker has to do more and more for less and less. It explains why families are devastated by divorce and neighbors are squabbling over the fence that separates their properties. It explains why church leaders get caught up in sexual and financial scandals. It even explains the tedium of domestic chores such as washing the dishes and doing the laundry.

The doctrine of sin also explains the greater evils of the wider world, as depravity works its way into the structures of society. The doctrine of sin explains our constant disappointment with the government, which always seems to be part of the problem, not just the solution. It explains why abortion has become virtually the sacrament of postmodern bioethics. It explains why slavery remains a worldwide scourge through human trafficking, especially for the sex trade. It explains why killers attack schoolchildren with automatic weapons. It explains why the forces of darkness gather in urban communities. It explains why street children are living in the sewers of Mongolia, the subways of Romania, the slums of Mexico City, and the garbage dumps of Calcutta. The doctrine of sin explains the famine and disease that afflict large parts of Asia and Africa. It explains the endless and seemingly intractable hostility in the Middle East and the persecution of the worldwide church. We should not be surprised by all this suffering. Sin is not only personal but also communal, and thus its influence is pervasive.

Worldviews themselves are part of the problem. Whether it is Communism's elimination of the human soul, Hinduism's denial of human dignity to the lower castes, or Islam's belief that evil is grounded in the character of God, worldviews have consequences—in these examples, to the detriment of human flourishing.

The same is true of modern secularism. As missiologist David Bosch has explained, this influential worldview elevates human reason over religious faith, treats creation as a closed system of natural causality, regards knowledge as fact based and therefore value free, assigns religion to the realm of personal opinion rather than objective truth, and prioritizes individual liberty over community life.[12] This way of seeing the world has had pervasively harmful effects on Western culture and the wider world. It has problematized moral instruction for higher education, removed religion from the public square, and made personal autonomy a higher goal than the common good.

Nor are Christians immune from these kinds of criticisms. To be consistent, our doctrine of sin needs to confess our own depravity. This includes all the ways that we fail to live up to the high standards of the character of Jesus Christ, all the ways we adapt to the world's way of thinking, and all the ways we use the Christian worldview as a weapon of cultural warfare. Having the right view of the world is not the only thing that matters. What really counts is living in love. But sadly, as Christians we do more than believe in sin; we also practice it.

THE WAGES OF SIN

There is more. There is also mortality, because the wages of sin, finally, is death (Rom. 6:23). Death was the penalty that God first threatened for disobedience in the garden of Eden: "When you eat

---

[12] See David J. Bosch, *Transforming Mission: Paradigm Shifts in Theology of Mission* (Maryknoll, NY: Orbis, 1991), chap. 9.

from it you will certainly die" (Gen. 2:17 NIV). Now we are mortal; having sinned in Adam, we also die in Adam (1 Cor. 15:21–22). We are dead spiritually—dead in our trespasses and sins (Eph. 2:1). One day soon we will die physically, not simply because death is a part of life in the natural universe but also because God stands in judgment against our sin. Our inescapable mortality is the irrefutable demonstration that we are sinners who seek our own ungodly glory. Nothing is more un-godlike than death, which strips away every last pretension to deity. Here is the futility of our condition: we will end up right back where we started. Rather than subduing the earth, we will be subdued by it, for dust we are, and to the dust we will return (Gen. 3:19).

For those who die without Christ, there will be a second death, infinitely and eternally more terrible than the first (Rev. 20:14–15). As a holy judge, God will display his wrath against sin. Though it offends the sensibilities of the secular mind, the doctrine of hell as a place of endless torment and eternal separation from God is a plain biblical truth that was taught more by Jesus than anyone else in the pages of Scripture (e.g., Matt. 5:22; 10:28; Luke 12:5; 15:22–23). Sin leads to death, and after that, to judgment.

If the best explanation for the beauty of humanity is the biblical doctrine of creation, then the best explanation for the tragedy of humanity is the biblical doctrine of sin. As he wrestles with the mystery of our humanity, the Princeton theologian Daniel Migliore writes that "we are rational and irrational, civilized and savage, capable of deep friendship and murderous hostility, free and in bondage, the pinnacle of creation and its greatest danger. We are Rembrandt and Hitler, Mozart and Stalin, Antigone and Lady Macbeth, Ruth and Jezebel."[13] What accounts best for our divided hearts is our fall from created innocence to sinful corruption. "This is the source and explanation of all that is wrong with

---

[13] Daniel L. Migliore, *Faith Seeking Understanding: An Introduction to Christian Theology*, 2nd ed. (Grand Rapids, MI: Eerdmans, 2004), 139.

man and the world he inhabits," wrote Philip Edgcumbe Hughes: "It is the sickness unto death from which man in his fallenness inescapably suffers."[14] Separated from God by our sin, we do not love him, worship him, obey him, or serve him as we should. Such is the depth of our fall that sin has become the pervasive and perverse condition of every human enterprise.

It all seems to be lost: the family, the church, the city, and the society that God intended—the science and technology, the law and the politics, the business and the arts. The world is the way it is, and we are the way we are, because we have fallen into sin. As a result, the heart of humanity has a deep and painful longing to return to paradise. Happiness is not only our hope, wrote G. K. Chesterton, "but also in some strange manner a memory; we are all kings in exile."[15] As Joni Mitchell set our longing to music in her 1969 song "Woodstock":

> We are stardust
> We are golden
> And we've got to get ourselves
> Back to the garden.

---

[14] Philip Edgcumbe Hughes, *The True Image: The Origin and Destiny of Man in Christ* (Leicester: Inter-Varsity, 1989), 136.
[15] G. K. Chesterton, *As I Was Saying*, ed. Robert Knille (Grand Rapids, MI: Eerdmans, 1985), 160.

+ 5

A WORK IN PROGRESS

Despite the doleful consequences of human depravity, all is not lost. In fact, knowing what the problem is helps us to see the solution. The problem with humanity is sin—our natural propensity to love ourselves and live for our glory rather than to love God and seek his glory. But when we finally become convinced of our lost and sinful condition—with all its deadly consequences—then we cry out for the kind of help that only God can give, saying, "What must [we] do to be saved?" (Acts 16:30).

DIVINE INTERVENTION

By now it should be clear that the answer cannot lie anywhere in us. If anything, human beings are only getting deeper in difficulty. What we need is for God to come and save us. And this is what God does, for "salvation belongs to the LORD" (Ps. 3:8; see also Jonah 2:9). Although nature can teach us about creation and the fall, it is only in the Bible that we learn the simple truth of redemption by grace: "Believe in the Lord Jesus, and you will be saved" (Acts 16:31). This faith-based approach to salvation stands in sharp contrast to religions that rely on human effort, including versions of Christianity that in any way make good works part of the basis for salvation.

Like creation, redemption is the work of the triune God. Together the Father, the Son, and the Spirit take the loving initiative to work their eternal plan for the redemption of our lost and fallen world. Yet the primary agent of our redemption is God the Son. The salvation appointed by the Father and applied by the Spirit is accomplished by the Son. This is the grand theme of Scripture: salvation in Jesus Christ. If Genesis 1 and 2 are primarily about creation, and Genesis 3 describes the fall, then the rest of the Bible chiefly is about the love and grace God has for sinners through the person and work of his Son. The compassion of God's saving plan is perhaps most perfectly expressed in the words of Jesus himself: "For God so loved the world, that he gave his only Son, that whoever believes in him should not perish but have eternal life. For God did not send his Son into the world to condemn the world, but in order that the world might be saved through him" (John 3:16–17).

In order to do this saving work, Jesus first entered the world that he had made and suffered the misery of its fallen condition. The same Son of God who created and sustains the universe "ultimately and permanently joined that creation in order to redeem it."[1] In his incarnation, which began with his miraculous conception in the womb of the Virgin Mary and became public with his birth at Bethlehem, God the Son became fully human as well as fully divine and thus experienced our embodied existence. The perfect and permanent unity of humanity and deity in Jesus Christ places God's imprimatur on physical life in a physical world. "When God in Jesus Christ claims space in the world," explained Dietrich Bonhoeffer, "even space in a stable because 'there was no other place in the inn'—God embraces the whole reality of the world in this narrow space and reveals its ultimate foundation."[2] Writing in the seventh century, John of Damascus described the attitude a follower of Christ should take toward God and toward his creation as a result:

> I do not worship matter, I worship the Creator of matter who
> became matter for my sake, who willed to take his abode in

---

[1] Duane A. Litfin, *Conceiving the Christian College* (Grand Rapids, MI: Eerdmans, 2004), 44.
[2] Dietrich Bonhoeffer, *Ethics*, Dietrich Bonhoeffer Works, vol. 6, ed. Clifford Green (Minneapolis: Fortress, 2005), 63.

matter; who worked out my salvation through matter. Never will I cease honoring the matter that wrought my salvation. I honor it, but not as God. . . . Because of this I salute all remaining matter with reverence, because God has filled it with his grace and power. Through it my salvation has come to me.[3]

In his humanity, Jesus did what God demanded, perfectly obeying the law and thereby fulfilling the covenant that we had broken in Adam. Although Jesus himself was never a sinner, he nevertheless endured the sufferings and sorrows of life in a fallen world, including weakness, pain, grief, cruelty, persecution, abuse, torture, and finally death. Thus we have a God who fully understands what it is like for us to endure all the troubles and tribulations of our present existence in a world that is marred by sin.

More than that, Jesus actually did something to address our fallen condition. "It is this body of our suffering that Christ was born into," wrote Wendell Berry, "to suffer it Himself and to fill it with light, so that beyond the suffering we can imagine Easter morning."[4] Jesus took on our life in order to take us into his life, achieving salvation through his crucifixion and bodily resurrection. When Jesus was crucified at Calvary, he took upon himself the punishment that we deserve, suffering God's holy wrath and righteous curse against our sin. The manner of Christ's death is significant. Under Jewish law, a crucified man was cursed by God (Deut. 21:22–23). This is perplexing, because as a sinless man Jesus did not deserve to be cursed. The New Testament resolves this conundrum by explaining that Jesus was cursed for *our* sin rather than his own. He died in our place. By his willing and perfect sacrifice, the full price for our sins was paid, and we no longer stand under the condemnation of God. With his blood, Jesus atoned for our sins and redeemed us for God.

---

[3] John of Damascus, quoted in James A. Nash, *Loving Nature: Ecological Integrity and Christian Responsibility* (Nashville: Abingdon, 1991), 109.
[4] Wendell Berry, *Hannah Coulter* (Berkeley, CA: Counterpoint, 2004), 171.

Then on the third day Jesus was raised again, coming back from the dead with the splendor of an immortal body and the power of eternal life. The good news of salvation—the gospel of grace—is that Jesus died on the cross for sinners and rose again from the grave. This was a bodily resurrection, in which the physical corpse of Jesus returned from the dead in miraculous glory. This proved that his sacrifice for our sins was accepted by God and brought immortality to humanity.

PERSONAL FAITH

Now, by the power of his resurrection, Jesus restores and renews all that humanity has lost through the fall of Adam. In the words of Saint Hippolytus, when Christ was raised from the dead and ascended to heaven, "His divine spirit gave life and strength to the tottering world, and the whole universe became stable once more, as if the stretching out, the agony of the Cross, had in some way gotten into everything."[5] Through the saving work of Jesus Christ, God brings us from sin to grace, from alienation to reconciliation, from death to eternal life.

The way we receive the multidimensional blessings of salvation is simply by faith in Jesus Christ. Since Jesus has fulfilled God's covenant, the only thing required of us is to trust in what Jesus has done. Once we are joined to Jesus by faith, united to him by the Holy Spirit, everything that is his becomes ours. As Calvin explained:

> We must understand that as long as Christ remains outside of us, and we are separated from him, all that he has suffered and done for the salvation of the human race remains useless and of no value for us. Therefore, to share with us what he has received from the Father, he had to become ours and to dwell within us. . . . We also, in turn, are said to be "engrafted into him"

---

[5] Saint Hippolytus, quoted in Charles Colson and Nancy Pearcey, *How Now Shall We Live?* (Wheaton, IL: Tyndale, 1999), 13.

(Rom. 11:17), and to "put on Christ" (Gal. 3:27); for, as I have
said, all that he possesses is nothing to us until we grow into one
body with him.[6]

As we are united to Christ, we find God's solution for all the
problems of our sin—the same problems we considered in the
previous chapter. The atoning sacrifice that Jesus made on the
cross took away our guilt by paying the penalty that we deserved.
Now that the guilt of our sin has been removed, we are no longer estranged from God but have fellowship with him: "While we
were enemies we were reconciled to God by the death of his Son"
(Rom. 5:10). We also experience reconciliation at the human level,
as the grace of God comforts our loneliness by enabling us to live
with others in love. Best of all, through the cross and the empty
tomb we have victory over our last and most fatal enemy: death
(1 Cor. 15:55–56). By the grace of God, we know that "God did
not appoint us to suffer wrath but to receive salvation through our
Lord Jesus Christ" (1 Thess. 5:9 NIV). This means that our fellowship with God will never come to an end but last forever.

Many Christians tend to think of salvation primarily in personal terms, and of course the grace God gives in Jesus Christ
is for us as individuals. I am the person whom Jesus has saved
through the cross and the empty tomb. I am the guilty sinner who
has been declared righteous before God in my justification. I am
the orphan who has been adopted as a son or daughter into my
Father's house. I am the unholy person who is being sanctified by
the renewing work of the Holy Spirit. I am the fractured image of
God who is being transformed into the beautiful likeness of Jesus
Christ and thereby restored and recreated in the image of my creator (Col. 3:10). I am the fallen creature whose body will be raised
up at the last day and physically glorified with immortal splendor.

---

[6] John Calvin, *Institutes of the Christian Religion*, ed. John T. McNeill; trans. Ford Lewis Battles;
Library of Christian Classics, 20–21 (Philadelphia: Westminster, 1960), 3.1.1.

This is the testimony of every person who comes to God through faith in Jesus Christ.

By the grace of God, I am also the person who is growing more and more to love the things that God calls me to love. The Holy Spirit is conforming my desires to the heart of Christ. At the same time, I am learning to think Christianly in every field of inquiry. God is transforming me by the renewing of my mind (Rom. 12:2), enabling me to take every thought captive in obedience to Christ (2 Cor. 10:5). The only way to gain a full understanding of any aspect of life is to view it through the lens of the gospel. Thus part of God's gracious work in my life is to teach me how to view the universe and everything in it from the perspective of the cross and the empty tomb.

In one of her poems Luci Shaw asks whether the cross where Jesus died is "high enough for a world view."[7] The answer is yes: the saving work of Jesus elevates our perspective, giving us a vantage point from which to see the world in God's true perspective. Put another way, the death and resurrection of Jesus enable the death and resurrection of the Christian mind. The Holy Spirit who raised Jesus from the dead is working in me to restore the knowledge of God, of myself, and of the world that I lost through the fall. Now I can see things the way I ought to see them—the way God sees them. Thus the formation of a Christian worldview itself is a gift of God's saving grace—a gift that is given to those who trust the written and incarnate Word of God.

COSMIC REDEMPTION

The new life that God has for us in Christ goes far beyond our personal salvation. The saving transformation that God works in us by his Spirit also has an influence on others as we become part of a new community of people who are forgiven in Christ. Grace is not merely personal but also communal. We are saved as the church

---

[7] Luci Shaw, "Craftsman," in *The Secret Trees* (Wheaton, IL: Harold Shaw, 1976), 59.

and not simply as individual Christians. In fact, all of the metaphors that the New Testament uses to describe our connection to Christ are corporate: he is the vine, we are the branches (John 15:5); he is the cornerstone, we are the building blocks (1 Pet. 2:4–6); he is the head, we are the members of his body (Eph. 4:15–16); and so forth. Our corporate identity is reinforced by the sacraments. In the name of the Father, the Son, and the Holy Spirit we are all baptized into one body. In the Lord's Supper (also called "Communion" or "the Eucharist") we eat one loaf and drink one cup—the thanksgiving meal of our salvation. It is only together that we can do what we were designed and destined to do: worship in community. Then together we go out to extend the kingdom of God—that is to say, the rule of God—by sharing the good news about Jesus Christ and serving people who are suffering the debilitating and alienating effects of the fall. As people of the new creation, we live out our faith in the ruins of the first creation.

The crucifixion and resurrection of Jesus have implications for everything. God's ultimate goal is nothing less than the redemption of the entire cosmos. Right now the creation itself is groaning under the weight of our sin, but this is only temporary, not eternal: "For the creation waits with eager longing for the revealing of the sons of God. For the creation was subjected to futility, not willingly, but because of him who subjected it, in hope that the creation itself will be set free from its bondage to corruption and obtain the freedom of the glory of the children of God" (Rom. 8:19–21). Redemption is not separate from creation but its intended destiny. It is the very world that God once made—now lost and fallen in sin—that God has a purpose to redeem. His plan does not call for simply destroying the universe but rather for "salvaging a sin-wrecked creation" and eventually establishing a new heavens and a new earth (see 2 Pet. 3:11–13).[8]

---

[8] David K. Naugle, *Worldview: The History of a Concept* (Grand Rapids, MI: Eerdmans, 2002), 284.

Jesus Christ is at the very center of this redemptive plan. It is in Christ that "all things hold together" (Col. 1:17), and it is through Christ that God is reconciling "to himself all things" (Col. 1:20). Jesus Christ now sits on the throne of heaven and rules over everything in the universe for the glory of God. This great truth inspired Abraham Kuyper to say, "There is not a square inch in the whole domain of our human existence over which Christ, who is Sovereign over *all*, does not cry: 'Mine!'"[9]

If Christ is preeminent, ruling over all things for the glory of God, then we are called to acknowledge his supreme lordship in all of life, every aspect of which is sacred to God. We are not called simply to trust in Jesus for our salvation but also to live for him in everything we do. As the perfect image of God—as "the radiance of the glory of God and the exact imprint of his nature" (Heb. 1:3)—Jesus shows us what we were meant to be. A person who follows him, wrote the Princeton theologian B. B. Warfield, should thus resolve "that God shall be God to him in all his thinking, feeling and willing—in the entire compass of his life activities, intellectual, moral and spiritual—throughout all his individual social and religious relations."[10] Elsewhere Warfield wrote about the emotional life of our Lord as the pattern for Christian feelings.[11] This is simply one example of the influence that the person of Christ should have on every dimension of Christian experience. In dedicating our lives to the service of Christ, we embrace his heart for the world and become agents of his redemption.

God is doing his gracious, redemptive work in two distinct ways. In a general sense, he is working through everything that happens, including what happens in the lives of people who do not explicitly acknowledge his sovereignty. Theologians call this "common

---

[9] Abraham Kuyper, "Sphere Sovereignty," in *Abraham Kuyper: A Centennial Reader*, ed. James D. Bratt (Grand Rapids, MI: Eerdmans, 1998), 488.

[10] Benjamin Breckinridge Warfield, *Calvin as a Theologian and Calvinism Today*, quoted in A. N. Martin, *The Practical Implications of Calvinism* (Edinburgh: Banner of Truth, 1979), 4.

[11] Benjamin Breckinridge Warfield, "The Emotional Life of Our Lord," in *The Person and Work of Christ*, ed. Samuel G. Craig (Philadelphia: Presbyterian and Reformed, 1950), 93–148.

grace"—common in the sense that it is universal. God has not given all his gifts or all his grace only to Christians. As the Scripture says, "The LORD is good to all, and his mercy is over all that he has made" (Ps. 145:9). Or again, "Every good gift and every perfect gift is from above" (James 1:17), which evidently includes the gifts that God gives to people who do not claim to follow Christ as well as to the people who do. "Since all truth is of God," wrote John Calvin, "if any ungodly man has said anything true, we should not reject it, for it also has come from God."[12] And according to James Davison Hunter, "People of every creed and no creed have talents and abilities, possess knowledge, wisdom, and inventiveness, and hold standards of goodness, truth, justice, morality, and beauty that are, in relative degree, in harmony with God's will and purposes."[13]

This means that God accomplishes his gracious purpose in the world through non-Christians as well as Christians. Their work also brings glory to God, even if that is not their explicit intent. Art and science both belong to the realm of common grace, where God is constantly at work.[14] In this sense, at least, a man like Wolfgang Amadeus Mozart (who for most of his life was not a practicing Christian) brought as much glory to God through his music as a man like Johann Sebastian Bach (who signed many of his compositions with the letters "sDg," meaning "to God alone be the glory"). This is not to deny the profound difference between the heart motivation of a writer or composer who wants to honor God and a person who doesn't. Their motivations may well affect the quality of their work in tangible as well as intangible ways. Yet the gifts of the unbeliever still honor the God who gave them. To give another example, the intellectual work that secular scholars

[12] John Calvin, 2 *Corinthians, Timothy, Titus and Philemon*, Calvin's New Testament Commentaries, vol. 10, ed. David W. Torrance and Thomas F. Torrance, trans. T. A. Smail (Grand Rapids, MI: Eerdmans, 1996), 364.

[13] James Davison Hunter, *To Change the World* (New York: Oxford University Press, 2010), 232.

[14] Abraham Kuyper develops this perspective in *Wisdom and Wonder: Common Grace in Science and Art*, ed. Jordan J. Ballor and Stephen J. Grabill, trans. Nelson D. Kloosterman (Grand Rapids, MI: Christian's Library Press, 2011).

do in a field such as neuroscience can be just as true to reality as the work that Christian scholars do (if not more so, in many cases).

Our commitment to seeing all truth as God's truth compels us to see the truth as it is, wherever it is, and not simply to dismiss what people say simply because they do not hold to a Christian worldview. Rather, we test what people say according to the truth that God has revealed in the world and in his Word, both written and incarnate. The doctrine that explains how non-Christians are able to teach the truth in many areas—and thus legitimates broad study in everything from music theory to organic chemistry—is the doctrine of common grace. By engaging with the best human minds in a wide range of academic disciplines and then connecting their insights to the truths of Scripture, Christians in the arts and sciences can help the church understand God and his work in the world more clearly.

To go a step farther, we also see God's grace at work in and through the many cultures of the world. No one is immune from the fall, of course, so the Christian worldview provides the basis for showing how every culture is fallen. But if it is true that every gift comes from God, then we should expect to see signs of his goodness in every tribe and tongue and nation. Every culture's history recounts stories of God's providence. Every culture's art reflects aspects of the created order as they have been perceived by particular people in a particular place. And every culture's people—with their common physical traits and characteristic attitudes—bear witness to the image of God in humanity. According to the doctrine of common grace, these are all gifts from God that deserve our appreciation through gaining fluency in foreign languages, building cross-cultural relationships, and acquiring the skills of sociology and anthropology. The more we learn about different people, the more we learn about what God is doing in the world and the better equipped we are to serve.

Still, common grace is not saving grace, and the blessings that come with creation fall well short of full redemption: they will not bring anyone into eternal life. Common grace relates to life in the present world, with or without a loving relationship with God through Jesus Christ. Saving grace, on the other hand, brings people into a personal friendship with the living God that lasts forever. So, in addition to giving everyone his common grace, Jesus has given his followers what is usually called "the Great Commission," sending us out into the world to preach the gospel of salvation. Jesus said, "All authority in heaven and on earth has been given to me. Go therefore and make disciples of all nations, baptizing them in the name of the Father and of the Son and of the Holy Spirit, teaching them to observe all that I have commanded you" (Matt. 28:18–20). We fulfill this commission by proclaiming the good news about the death and resurrection of Jesus Christ with the goal of rescuing people from sin and bringing them into a state of grace before they go on to glory. This proclamation should never be manipulative or coercive. Rather, as an expression of Christlike love that takes a genuine interest in the well-being of other persons, we tell people the truth about Jesus and invite them to join us in following him.

Notice that this Great Commission includes teaching people who choose to follow Christ how to obey *everything* that God has commanded (v. 20). The Great Commission encompasses the transmission of a complete Christian worldview, the total salvation that God is bringing into the world. When God tells us to teach people "all" that he has commanded, this includes teaching them God's view of the world. Christians do not have to choose between evangelism and cultural engagement, therefore. It is both/and, not either/or. By taking such a comprehensive view of what we need to teach the world, the Great Commission renews our cultural mandate.[15] As Christians we are called to do something more than help save people's souls; we are also called to influence the

---

[15] Gregory Johnson, *The World according to God: A Biblical View of Culture, Work, Science, Sex, and Everything Else* (Downers Grove, IL: InterVarsity, 2002), 177.

thinking of our culture. This highlights the value of higher education that is surrendered to the lordship of Jesus Christ, empowered by his grace, and extended to every dimension of human thought: "When the Father awakens us by his sovereign Spirit, we draw from Christ's life the resurrection power that enables us to love God's world, even as we await its full restoration."[16]

REVERSE THE CURSE

God's redemptive grace is working in us and through us to restore all the things that were given in creation but lost in the fall. His purposes for redemption are as extensive as his purposes were in creation. Though fallen, every dimension of human experience is redeemable, and our calling as Christians is part of God's redemptive work in the world. By the grace of God in Christ, we recover the heart's "high and holy calling to consecrate every department of life and every energy at its disposal to the glory of God."[17] And despite our many failings, by the gracious work of the Holy Spirit we are able to make substantial progress in restoring things to their created intention. Here is how Francis Bacon—the father of the scientific method—described our calling within the redemptive purposes of God: "Man by the Fall fell at the same time from his state of innocence and from his dominion over nature. Both of these losses, however, can even in this life be in some part repaired; the former by religion and faith, the latter by the arts and sciences."[18]

This high calling to repair the ruins of the fall works itself out in all of the areas of life that are damaged and distorted by sin. Now, by the grace of God, we are able to worship God in Spirit and in truth, celebrating the beauty of his holiness with reverence and joy. Whether we worship God in private acts of devotion or in the public services of the church, the presence of grace enables us to glorify God. We are able to live as moral beings in a moral universe,

---

[16] Ibid., 13.
[17] Abraham Kuyper, *Lectures on Calvinism* (1931; repr. Grand Rapids, MI: Eerdmans, 1994), 24.
[18] Francis Bacon, *Novum Organum Scientiarum* (1620).

keeping the law of God (albeit imperfectly). Every time we show respect to our elders, or help preserve an innocent life, or give generously to the poor, we show how the grace of God has reoriented our moral compass. We are able to honor God with our bodies—treating them as temples for the Holy Spirit and using them as instruments of righteousness. This means more than avoiding destructive behaviors; it also means becoming the hands and the feet of Christ in serving others. Honoring God with our bodies includes our sexuality, which finds its truest freedom and highest pleasure in the sex of joy. The holy gifts of purity and chastity are available to everyone. Whether married or single, and regardless of the orientation of our sexual desires, all of us can honor God by submitting to his gracious purposes for our sexuality: joyful abstinence for singles and sexual giving for married couples.

Even the physical sufferings we endure—such as disability and disease—have an ultimately redemptive purpose, as God uses evil to accomplish our good and his glory (Rom. 8:28). This last point needs to be underscored because it is so commonly misunderstood. God's purpose for us in this life is not simply to make us happy. If this were his purpose, then—as many critics have pointed out—he seems to be failing miserably. But in fact God has deeper purposes. This life is a proving ground to show us our need for him and to begin a transformation that will not be made complete until the perfect happiness of the life to come.

Another place where grace enables us to give honor to Christ is in the home life of our marriages and families, as the Holy Spirit reconciles broken relationships and enables us to fulfill our domestic responsibilities with gentle godliness. Though painful in itself, childbearing becomes a gracious means for God to build his kingdom from one generation to the next. As a mother sings praise songs for the baby in her arms, or as a father reads the Bible to his family at dinnertime, the Christian worldview is formed in the hearts and minds of future leaders.

By grace we honor God in our communities, noticing our neighbors' needs and seeking to build relationships that will help them flourish. We also *work* for the glory of God, serving him as a redeemed person in our regular calling—whatever job God has given us to do each day. Jesus himself has become our client and our boss, for, as the Scripture says, "whatever you do, work heartily, as for the Lord and not for men, knowing that from the Lord you will receive the inheritance as your reward. You are serving the Lord Christ" (Col. 3:23–24). The phrase "whatever you do" reminds us that the promises God makes to godly workers extend to every legitimate calling. In this respect, there is essentially no difference between secular work and so-called Christian ministry: they both have God's blessing. As Gerard Manley Hopkins wrote:

> It is not only prayer that gives God glory but work. Smiting on an anvil, sawing a beam, whitewashing a wall, driving horses, sweeping, scouring, everything gives God some glory if being in his grace you do it as your duty. To go to communion worthily gives God great glory, but a man with a dungfork in his hand, a woman with a slop pail, give him glory too. He is so great that all things give him glory if you mean they should.[19]

Now by grace we are able to care for our world, cultivating its fruit and savoring its bounty while at the same time protecting its resources and sharing them with people in greater need. The church is (or at least ought to be) characterized by using what we have for others rather than for ourselves, thereby dethroning money from its idolatrous throne in a materialistic society. We pursue social and personal justice, showing local and global concern for the poor and the persecuted and employing righteous power and generous giving on their behalf under the authority of God. To be clear, we do not seize power for ourselves, especially political

[19] Gerard Manley Hopkins, from "The Principle or Foundation," an address based on *The Spiritual Exercises of St. Ignatius Loyola*, in *Ordinary Graces: Christian Teaching on the Interior Life*, ed. Lorraine Kisly (New York: Bell Tower, 2000), 170.

power. Yet we do hope to be what the sociologist James Davison Hunter wisely calls a "faithful presence" wherever God calls us to serve, leaving the influence of our service in the hands of God.[20]

What else does God's grace enable us to do in the world? Now we are able to pursue science within the constraints of holy wisdom and business within the bonds of charity, producing goods, creating value, and earning profit for the benefit of other people. We are able to sing, sculpt, play music, and produce films to the glory of God, being realistic about the pain and ugliness of fallen humanity while at the same time remaining joyful in the hope and beauty of redemption. While the arts hover "between life and death, despair and hope," they also "point to, or even redefine, the world to come, causing us to rise up, like Lazarus, from the dank tomb of cynicism and despair."[21] We are also able to play sports and pursue hobbies in ways that build relationships and bring refreshment to our bodies and souls. And we are able to work at building and governing the great cities that God always intended for us to build—not for our glory but for his majesty, as every aspect of life finds its fulfillment in loving community.

This is all part of God's gracious, redeeming work in the world—the building of the kingdom of God. It is not just our souls that God has a plan to save, but also our bodies, and with our bodies, the whole created order. We ourselves are part of the plan. Thus, we belong to what some Christians have called "a counterculture for the common good." As the church of Jesus Christ we participate in his redeeming work by fulfilling the Great Commission and the cultural mandate, thereby working out the implications of God's grace in all of life. Of course, no individual could possibly do everything that needs to be done for Christ and his kingdom in any one area of life, let alone all of them put together. None of us can carry the weight of the world. But each

---

[20] Hunter, *To Change the World*, 95.
[21] Makoto Fujimura, "The Aroma of the New," *Books and Culture* (July/August 2011): 37.

of us can and should do the things that God is calling us to do within our own sphere of influence, based on the gifts and opportunities that are unique to our situation in life. Because the gifts that Christ has given to each of us by the Spirit are complementary, as the church we are more than the sum of our parts. By the grace of God that reverses the curse of sin, we are called "in every domain" to "discover the treasures and develop the potencies hidden by God in nature and in human life."[22]

In keeping with this comprehensive vision of the kingdom of God, apologist Bill Edgar aptly summarizes the Christian worldview as having "trifocal" vision. Looking with the triple lens of creation, sin, and grace, we are able to perceive all three stages of redemptive history in our present experience. Edgar writes:

> First, the creation is still good, and its structures continue to function under God's care. Second, everything is distorted, fallen, so that the direction things should have taken is wrong, being diverted. But third, there is hope. As the seasons of revelation unfold, we find out more about all three, but especially about the nature of our hope, the gospel, the good news that in spite of sin, God has so loved us that sin will not have the last word.[23]

All three stages of redemptive history are presently in view. We see them simultaneously: what the world was made to be (in creation), what has become of it (because of sin), and what it may yet become (by the grace of God). This multidimensional perspective on reality explains why the Christian worldview is at one and the same time brutally honest about the troubles of life and unfailingly hopeful about what God will do.

---

[22] Kuyper, *Lectures on Calvinism*, 31.
[23] William Edgar, *Truth in All Its Glory: Commending the Reformed Faith* (Phillipsburg, NJ: P&R, 2004), 148.

✚ 6

PARADISE CONSUMMATED

Sin does not have the last word, because we live in the hope of a coming glory—the happiest of all endings.

One of the great mysteries of redemption is that in our current existence the high calling to glorify God is achieved only imperfectly. "At present," the Scripture says, "we do not yet see everything in subjection to [Christ]" (Heb. 2:8). God is busy doing what sometimes seems to be a slow work of grace in the world, and even within the community of God's people we see only glimpses of the glory that is waiting to be revealed. We see this at the personal level, in the gradual progress of our spiritual growth. The hopeful lament of the converted slave trader and famous hymn writer John Newton is the testimony of every Christian: "I am not what I ought to be; I am not what I wish to be; I am not what I hope to be. But blessed be God, I am not what I used to be, and by the grace of God I am what I am."[1] We see the same thing at the level of church, community, and culture, where God's redemptive work is under way. We are under grace but not yet in glory. The recovery of everything that creation lost in the fall is begun but not completed.

As a result, we are living in what theologians sometimes call the "already" and the "not yet." God has *already* accomplished our redemption in Christ, but he has *not yet* fulfilled all of the promises of his coming kingdom. To put this another way, we are living somewhere between the sufferings of the cross and the joy of

---

[1] John Newton, quoted in Alan Sell, *The Spirit of Our Life* (Boston, KY: Ragged Edge, 2000), 47.

the empty tomb. The dark decay of death is all around us because of sin; yet the dawn of the coming resurrection is lighting our way. Jesus has returned from the grave. As the risen Christ he is with us in our present suffering, and therefore we live in the hope of God's perfect future.

THE END OF THE WORLD

We have considered what it means for the followers of Christ to live by grace in a fallen world that is in the process of being redeemed. But what does the Christian worldview tell us about the perfect world that is yet to come?

We know that when we die we will enter the presence of God. This is a crucial question for any worldview: What happens when I die? Is there life after death? And if so, what kind of life is it? Hinduism says we are reincarnated as a different life form. Pantheism says we become one with the universe. Naturalism says we simply become extinct. People who believe this live only for the moment, giving little thought to their eternal destiny. But Christianity says that death is not the end; our present life has future consequences. The body will be laid in the dust for a time (this is the result of God's curse against our sin), but the soul returns to its maker. As the Scripture says, for the believer to be "away from the body" is also to be "at home with the Lord" (2 Cor. 5:8).

What else do we know about the future? We know that someday Jesus will return to planet earth. "I will come again and will take you to myself," Jesus said, "that where I am you may be also" (John 14:3). Jesus will come the way he left when he ascended to heaven, riding clouds of glory (Acts 1:9–11). This event—which the Bible often describes as "the coming" (e.g., 1 Thess. 3:13) or "the appearing" (e.g., 1 Tim. 6:14) of the Lord Jesus Christ—will bring all present earthly existence to an end. Some people doubt whether this is really true, but the Bible says that "by the same word the heavens and earth that now exist are stored up for fire, being kept until the day of judgment and destruction of the ungodly" (2 Pet. 3:7). On that day, which will come like a thief in the night, "the heavens will pass away with a roar, and the heavenly bodies will be burned up and dissolved, and the earth and the works that are done on it will be exposed" (2 Pet. 3:10). This universe is destined for destruction before restoration.

We also know that when Jesus comes again, he will come as the judge of the final judgment. There will be a righting of all wrongs and a balancing of all books, according to God's perfect justice. Every sin will be exposed. The Bible is straightforward about this: "God will bring every deed into judgment, with every secret thing, whether good or evil" (Eccles. 12:14; see also Rom. 2:16). There are no exceptions: "We must all appear before the judgment seat of Christ, so that each one may receive what is due for what he has done in the body, whether good or evil" (2 Cor. 5:10).

The prospect of coming judgment gives eternal significance to all our words and actions—everything from the casual criticism we make about a friend to where we travel in cyberspace. For those who die outside Christ—for those who persist in their sinful rebellion without ever coming to Jesus in faith and repentance— judgment will bring damnation. This damnation is crucial to the blessedness of heaven because it guarantees the end of everything evil. Wrongs must be rectified and the works of the Devil destroyed. Meanwhile, those who claim forgiveness through the cross and the empty tomb will be saved on the basis of the perfect righteousness of Jesus Christ; God will receive us unto himself. And all of this will be for the glory of God. The final judgment will demonstrate both the righteous holiness and the gracious mercy of Jesus Christ, who will return at the end of the ages "to be glorified in his holy people and to be marveled at among all those who have believed" (2 Thess. 1:10 NIV).

Only then—only when Jesus comes again—will the world

be all that God intends for it to become. And only then will *we* become all that God intends for *us* to be. This is the goal for which God has been working since eternity past. All things are not only *from* God but also *for* God—for his glory in Christ. This goal seemed to be frustrated by the fall, but God has not stopped working toward it, and he will reach it in the end. God is no more satisfied with this fallen world than we are, but unlike us he is able to redeem it, and he will. Jesus Christ must reign until all things are brought into subjection to him, and God becomes all in all (1 Cor. 15:25, 28). This is God's eternal plan, and when it comes to fruition, it will last forever. Once Paradise is regained, it can never be lost, which is one of the things that distinguishes the consummation from creation: it is indefectible.

NEW HEAVENS, NEW EARTH

If it is true that one day Jesus will reign supreme over everything, then salvation must be about something far grander than simply my own entrance into eternal life. The coming glory is cosmic in its scope, encompassing not only a new heaven but also "a new earth" (Rev. 21:1), as the creation is re-created in Christ and restored to its intended design. Paradise will not merely be regained in the world to come, but consummated. In this way, God will fulfill his ancient promise to make all things new: "For behold, I create new heavens and a new earth, and the former things shall not be remembered or come into mind. But be glad and rejoice forever in that which I create; for behold, I create Jerusalem to be a joy, and her people to be a gladness" (Isa. 65:17–18; see also Rev. 21:1).

By mentioning "Jerusalem," the Bible sets the promise of future joy in an explicitly urban context. History began in a garden (the garden of Eden), but it will end in a city (the garden city of the New Jerusalem). Here is how the apostle John described that blessed metropolis in his revelation of God's eternal kingdom:

> Then the angel showed me the river of the water of life, bright
> as crystal, flowing from the throne of God and of the Lamb
> through the middle of the street of the city; also, on either side
> of the river, the tree of life with its twelve kinds of fruit, yielding
> its fruit each month. The leaves of the tree were for the healing
> of the nations. (Rev. 22:1–2)

When we remember the calling we were given at creation—our
cultural mandate to realize the potentialities of the world that God
has made—and when we consider our deep need for community,
it makes perfect sense that we have an urban future. The city is the
place where people gather to make culture, and in the celestial city
of God all our relationships and activities will come together to
be what they were always intended to become. As Andy Crouch
has written,

> Our eternal life in God's recreated world will be the fulfillment
> of what God originally asked us to do: cultivating and creating
> in full and lasting relationship with our Creator. This time, of
> course, we will not just be tending a garden; we will be sustain-
> ing the life of a city, a harmonious human society that has devel-
> oped all the potentialities hidden in the original creation to their
> fullest. Culture—redeemed, transformed and permeated by the
> presence of God—will be the activity of eternity.[2]

The community life of that last and future city will not be dis-
continuous with our present experience but will be its completion
and consummation. It is the lost and fallen creation that God will
restore, redeem, and renew. In some mysterious way, the best things
from this life will be carried forward into the life to come. Thus
when the Bible envisions the coming kingdom of God, it promises
that "the kings of the earth will bring their glory into it . . . the
glory and the honor of the nations" (Rev. 21:24, 26). Even if we
do not understand the full implications of this promise, the Bible

---

[2] Andy Crouch, *Culture Making: Recovering Our Creative Calling* (Downers Grove, IL: InterVarsity, 2008), 173.

is making a clear connection between the present and the future, when the glory of the nations will become the glory of God.[3] Whatever good work we do for God is not lost but becomes part of his eternal kingdom. And this is true for all nations, as the diverse cultures of the world bring their unique gifts into the kingdom of God. The beauty of the creation around us and the art that we produce anticipate the coming of the glory of God. "With trembling hand," wrote Abraham Kuyper, the God-honoring artifacts of human culture "reach out toward the glory that through Christ will one day fill heaven and earth."[4] Jeremy Begbie is similarly optimistic about the potentiality of our creativity: "Whether through paint or sound, metaphor or movement, we are given the inestimable gift of participating in the re-creative work of the Triune God, anticipating that final and unimaginable re-creation of all matter, space, and time, the fulfillment of all things visible and invisible."[5]

The glory of Christ will include the redemption of our bodies. This is what Christians mean when we confess our faith in the resurrection *of the body*. It is not just our souls that God plans to redeem but also our bodies: "Our citizenship is in heaven, and from it we await a Savior, the Lord Jesus Christ, who will transform our lowly body to be like his glorious body, by the power that enables him even to subject all things to himself" (Phil. 3:20–21). The life to come is not immaterial and insubstantial but an embodied existence. Thus the implications of the incarnation and the resurrection are never-ending: eternal life is both physical and spiritual. God will redeem us as whole persons. In bodies raised and glorified like the immortal body of Jesus himself, we will enjoy resurrection life to the full, body and soul.

---

[3] See Richard Mouw, *When the Kings Come Marching In: Isaiah and the New Jerusalem*, rev. ed. (Grand Rapids, MI: Eerdmans, 2002).

[4] Abraham Kuyper, *Wisdom and Wonder: Common Grace in Science and Art*, ed. Jordan J. Ballor and Stephen J. Grabill, trans. Nelson D. Kloosterman (Grand Rapids, MI: Christian's Library Press, 2011), 144.

[5] Jeremy Begbie, "The Future: Looking to the Future: A Hopeful Subversion," in *For the Beauty of the Church: Casting a Vision for the Arts*, ed. W. David O. Taylor (Grand Rapids, MI: Baker, 2010), 181.

Glory will also bring the redemption of our relationships. In the new heavens and the new earth we will live in perfect harmony, peace, and justice as the new family of God. Old hostilities will be set aside, and broken relationships will be reconciled. The lion will lie down with the lamb (Isa. 11:6). Swords will be beaten into plowshares (Mic. 4:3). The community lost by sin will be perfectly restored. Together we will work for the glory of God and find the perfection of our play. One of the happiest promises in all of Scripture is the one Zechariah made about the New Jerusalem: "The streets of the city shall be full of boys and girls playing in its streets" (Zech. 8:5). The Bible does not tell us what the children will be playing there. Maybe they will skip rope, or play tag, or ride scooters. Perhaps they will play soccer or stickball. The Bible does not dwell on the details but gives us enough of a glimpse to know that God's everlasting kingdom will be a place of perfect peace and playful joy.

What can we say about the repristination (or perfect restoration) of all the other areas of life that were made good in creation, lost in the fall, and have begun to be restored by grace? When glory comes, everything will be renewed, and we will be called to display the possibilities of the new creation in every dimension of human culture.

Imagine, for example, what discoveries of science we shall make in the new heavens and the new earth! One of the first impulses we have in any new place is to explore our surroundings. Surely this desire will carry over in to the life to come, when we will want to learn everything there is to know about the physical makeup of the new heavens and the new earth. As theologian Dallas Willard has explained, "God himself loves the earth dearly and never takes his hands off it. And because he loves it and it is good, our care of it is also eternal work and part of our eternal life."[6]

---

[6] Dallas Willard, *The Divine Conspiracy* (San Francisco: HarperCollins, 1997), 205.

Then imagine what music we will make, what paintings, and what poetry! All of the arts will flourish as they fully achieve their true and creative goal of bringing glory to our good, true, and beautiful God. If we believe "that there will be a new Jerusalem," writes Abraham Kuyper, "located on a new earth, under a new heaven, then art is a preliminary scintillation already in this earthly life of what is coming."[7]

In her prize-winning novel *Gilead*, Marilynne Robinson draws an analogy that offers a compelling vision of art and life in the everlasting city of God. According to Robinson's lead character, "In eternity this world will be Troy, and all that has passed here will be the epic of the universe, the ballad they sing in the streets."[8] The novelist thus anticipates that the heroic deeds of this life will be remembered and celebrated in the life to come. Further, she presents heaven as a place for writing and singing, where public art is a daily part of community life. What happens in this life ultimately becomes the subject of the next life's lyric poetry—"the ballad they sing in the streets." Art is for eternity.

We have so much to look forward to. But what is most important about our eternal destiny is God himself and the worship of God. In his vision of glory, the apostle John described the concentric circles of angels and saints that even now gather around the throne of God. This too is part of the already and the not yet: the worship that has started in heaven and will never end. At the very center of heaven's praise is the infinitely glorious person of the Lord Jesus Christ, receiving universal worship and absolute praise:

> Then I looked, and I heard around the throne and the living creatures and the elders the voice of many angels, numbering myriads of myriads and thousands of thousands, saying with a loud voice, "Worthy is the Lamb who was slain, to receive power and wealth and wisdom and might and honor and glory

[7] Abraham Kuyper, *Wisdom and Wonder*, 145.
[8] Marilynne Robinson, *Gilead* (New York: Farrar, Strauss, Giroux, 2004), 57.

and blessing!" And I heard every creature in heaven and on earth and under the earth and in the sea, and all that is in them, saying, "To him who sits on the throne and to the Lamb be blessing and honor and glory and might forever and ever!" (Rev. 5:11–13)

This was God's goal for us from the beginning: that we would know the joy of worshiping him. It is why God created all things and why he is redeeming us from our lost and fallen condition. The universe created *by* Christ and *through* Christ is also *for* Christ, so that he may receive all of the glory that he alone deserves. The Christian worldview is liturgical as well as cerebral; it culminates with an everlasting crescendo of praise.

THE END FOR WHICH GOD CREATED THE WORLD

What difference does it make to know that we are made to praise, that we are destined to worship God through Jesus Christ? It makes all the difference in the world. The Dutch theologian G. C. Berkouwer explained that the message of the gospel is not merely spiritual "but good tidings applied to man's entire existence." The biblical expectation, he said, "includes the new earth, and the present life is founded on and proceeds from this expectation. Only with an eye to God's future can one understand the richness of life in the present."[9] In other words, the Christian view of glory enables us to see *everything* in the world in its true and total perspective. In all the pain of our fallen world we do not despair, but by the grace that is ours in Jesus Christ—and in the hope of his glory—we work together for the kingdom of God.

The story is sometimes told of a king who wanted to build a grand cathedral. When the work was well under way, the king went to visit the work site and began to ask the workers what they were doing. One man said that he was cutting a stone. His attention was narrowly focused on the task at hand. Another man said that he

---

[9] G. C. Berkouwer, *The Return of Christ* (Grand Rapids, MI: Eerdmans, 1972), 230.

was shaping a stone to complete an archway. He better understood how his job fit in with the work of others. But one man told the king that he was building a sanctuary for the glory of God. This was the man who had the greatest joy, because he had a deeper motivation for what he was doing. He had a worldview that connected his own particular calling to God's ultimate purpose for the entire universe. He understood what Jonathan Edwards called "the end for which God created the world"—namely, the glory of God.[10]

Do you understand the purpose for which you were made? Have you captured a Christ-centered vision of all things? Have you embraced your calling to glorify the triune God and to enjoy him forever in every dimension of human existence?

It takes a lifetime—more than that, an eternity—for anyone to work out all the implications of the Christian world- and life-view. What this looks like is different for each person, according to his or her unique background, gifts, personality, and calling. But having the right worldview makes all the difference for all of us, both for now and for eternity. It helps us understand the purpose for why God created the world and everything in it. It clarifies our perspective on the daily difficulty and distress of life in a fallen world. And it offers the hope of a future reality that shapes our present existence, until the day when Jesus comes again in triumph and says, "Behold, I am making all things new" (Rev. 21:5).

---

[10] Jonathan Edwards, *A Dissertation Concerning the End for Which God Created the World* (1765).

QUESTIONS FOR REFLECTION

1) How would you define "worldview"? What are some key questions that every worldview needs to answer?

2) Why is it important to be self-reflective about your worldview?

3) What is the creator/creature distinction? Why is this distinction basic to the Christian worldview?

4) What does creation teach us about who God is? About who Jesus is? About who we are?

5) What are some specific ways that God has created you to glorify him?

6) Briefly describe the main effects of humanity's fall into sin. In what areas of life or experience do the tragic consequences of sin affect you most deeply or directly?

7) What is "common grace"? What does this doctrine contribute to the formation of a Christian worldview? What are the limitations of common grace?

8) What is the connection between the Great Commission and the cultural mandate?

9) In what areas of life do you experience the tension between the "already" and the "not yet"—between the fact that Jesus has *already* been raised from the dead, but has *not yet* returned in the fullness of his glory?

10) For what purpose has God created the universe? How will this purpose be achieved in his eternal kingdom?

GLOSSARY

Agnosticism. Derived from the Greek words meaning "no" (*a*) and "knowledge" (*gnosis*), this term refers to a worldview or philosophy that claims it is impossible to know anything for certain about God.

Apologetics. The formal or systematic defense of the Christian faith, or of central doctrines such as the trustworthiness of Scripture or the historical reality of the crucifixion and resurrection of Jesus Christ, typically through rational argumentation.

Atheism. A worldview or philosophy that denies the existence of God and usually asserts that the material universe—which is the produce of chance—is the only form of existence.

Consummation. The end of human history at the second coming of Jesus Christ, with the resurrection of the dead, the final judgment, and the establishment of the eternal kingdom of God.

Covenant. A free act in which God graciously establishes a mutually binding relationship with his people, often through a representative. In making a covenant God promises certain blessings for obedience and threatens certain punishments for disobedience, although many biblical covenants offer unconditional blessings on the basis of God's unilateral promise to fulfill the terms of the covenant himself. Notable examples include God's covenants with Noah (Gen. 8:20–22), Abraham (Genesis 15; 17:1–14), Moses (Exodus 19), and David (2 Sam. 7:1–17), and the new covenant, which is fulfilled in Christ (Jer. 31:31–34; Luke 22:20).

Creation. The act of God in making the entire universe out of nothing (*ex nihilo*), simply by the word of his power. The term can also refer to the physical universe, as created by God.

Creation mandate. *See* cultural mandate.

Creed. Derived from the Latin word *credo*, meaning "I believe," a creed is a formal summary of Christian doctrine, expressed in the form of a personal or corporate confession (such as the Apostles' Creed).

Crucifixion. The common Roman method for executing the death penalty—as carried out against Jesus of Nazareth—in which the victim was nailed to a wooden cross and left to die, usually by asphyxiation. The pain of crucifixion was compounded by its shame. For the Romans, the cross was an instrument of public humiliation; for the Jews, it signified that the victim was cursed by God (Deut. 21:22–23; Gal. 3:13).

Cultural mandate. The injunction of Genesis 1:28, in which God, having created the world and everything in it, assigned to humanity the tasks of developing the inherent capacities of creation by filling, subduing, caring for, and ruling over the earth.

Depravity. The comprehensive moral corruption of human nature that arises from the fall of Adam and subjects every person to the bondage and penalty of sin.

Dualism. Any system of thought that divides everything into two fundamental realities, such as mind and body or good and evil.

Evolution. Most simply, change in the inherited characteristics of biological populations over successive generations. For many naturalists and materialists, evolution functions as a comprehensive theory of human origins, to the exclusion of a creator. For Christians, any changes in the natural world are subject to the sovereign providence of God.

Ex nihilo. A Latin expression meaning "out of nothing," which in Christianity refers to the doctrine of creation. God did not simply give order to eternally existing matter or fashion the universe out of his own divine being, but he created all things out of nothing.

Fall, the. The historical event in which Adam and Eve, as the first human beings and the representatives of the entire human race, disobeyed God's command not to eat from the tree of the knowledge of good and evil, thereby bringing sin and death upon humanity.

Glory (of God). The visual majesty of the presence of God, which is manifested most completely in the radiant splendor of the immortal body of the risen Christ. The term may also be used to refer to the weightiness of God's being and the inherent beauty of his divine attributes.

Gospel. The death and resurrection of Jesus Christ, resulting in the forgiveness of sins and the free gift of eternal life for anyone who trusts in him. The gospel has broader implications, too, including the creation of a new community through the Holy Spirit and the redemption of the entire universe. The term *Gospel* also refers to any of the four biblical books (Matthew, Mark, Luke, and John) that proclaim the true story of the birth, life, ministry, death, and resurrection of Jesus Christ.

Grace. The unmerited favor of God, especially as given to sinners through Jesus Christ.

Great Commission. The command Jesus gave his followers in Matthew 28:18–20 to go into the whole world and make disciples by proclaiming his gospel, baptizing all nations in the name of the triune God, and teaching all people everywhere to obey the will of God.

Imago Dei. The Latin term denoting the doctrine that human beings are created in the image and likeness of God.

Incarnation. The embodiment of God the Son in human form as Jesus Christ. In his incarnation, the divine nature of the Son was united with human nature in one person, Jesus Christ, who is both truly God and truly man forever.

Marxism. A materialist worldview based on the political and economic theories of Karl Marx in his critique of capitalism.

Materialism. Any worldview or philosophy that contends that physical matter is the only reality or form of existence.

Naturalism. Any worldview or philosophy that maintains that the natural universe of matter and energy is the only reality.

Noetic. Of or pertaining to knowledge, from the Greek word *gnosis.*

Original sin. Humanity's inherent propensity to sin and inclination to evil, which every person has inherited as a consequence of the fall of Adam in eating the forbidden fruit.

Pluralism. In philosophy, and in its most extreme form, the belief that all worldviews provide equally true, equally valid accounts of reality.

Post-Christian. A society—such as the United States, increasingly, or most of the nations of western Europe—in which Christianity is no longer recognized as the predominant worldview.

Postmodernism. Any worldview or philosophy that rejects modern explanations of the world. Postmodern thinkers typically deny the existence of objective truth, the possibility of transcendent meaning, and the validity of unifying metanarratives (such as Christianity) that attempt to provide a total explanation of reality.

Protestant Reformation (Reformation). The European Christian movement in the sixteenth century that transformed the doctrine, practices, and structures of the Roman Catholic Church. The Reformers defended Scripture alone (not human tradition) as the only ultimate authority for Christian doctrine and Christ alone received by faith alone (not good works) as the only means of the sinner's justification before God.

Redemption. To be delivered from sin through the saving work of Jesus Christ. More specifically, to be released from spiritual bondage through the payment that Jesus made for sin in his crucifixion.

Resurrection. Miraculously rising to everlasting life after death in bodily form, as Jesus did on the third day after his crucifixion, and as every true follower of Jesus will do at the final judgment.

Secular humanism. The belief that humanity is capable of flourishing in life, morality, and happiness without believing in God.

Sin. Any violation or transgression of the law of God, or failure to follow its precepts and principles.

Sovereignty. The divine power and kingly autonomy of God, who holds everything that happens under his absolute control.

Trinity. The biblical doctrine that there is one God in three persons: the Father, the Son, and the Holy Spirit.

Worldview. Briefly, the total perspective by which a person or a culture perceives and interprets the world.

RESOURCES FOR FURTHER STUDY

Bonzo, J. Matthew, and Michael Stevens, eds. *After Worldview: Christian Higher Education in Postmodern Worlds*. Sioux Center, IA: Dordt College Press, 2009.

Boston, Thomas. *Human Nature in Its Fourfold State*. In *The Complete Works of the Late Rev. Thomas Boston, vol. 8*. Edited by Samuel M'Millan. 12 vols. London, 1853. Repr. Wheaton, IL: Richard Owen Roberts, 1980.

Carson, D. A. *Christ and Culture Revisited*. Grand Rapids, MI: Eerdmans, 2008.

Carson, D. A., and John D. Woodbridge, eds. *God and Culture: Essays in Honor of Carl F. H. Henry*. Grand Rapids, MI: Eerdmans, 1993.

Colson, Charles, and Nancy Pearcey. *How Now Shall We Live?* Wheaton, IL: Tyndale, 1999.

Crouch, Andy. *Culture Making: Recovering Our Creative Calling*. Downers Grove, IL: InterVarsity, 2008.

Dockery, David S., ed. *Faith and Learning: A Handbook for Christian Higher Education*. Nashville: Broadman, 2012.

Dockery, David S., and Gregory Alan Thornbury. *Shaping a Christian Worldview: The Foundations of Christian Higher Education*. Nashville: Broadman, 2002.

Holmes, Arthur F. *Contours of a World View*. Grand Rapids, MI: Eerdmans, 1983.

Huffman, Douglas S., ed. *Christian Contours: How a Biblical Worldview Shapes the Mind and Heart*. Grand Rapids, MI: Kregel, 2011.

Johnson, Gregory. *The World according to God: A Biblical View of Culture, Work, Science, Sex, and Everything Else*. Downers Grove, IL: InterVarsity, 2002.

Kuyper, Abraham. *Wisdom and Wonder: Common Grace in Science and Art*. Translated by Nelson D. Kloosterman. Edited by Jordan J. Ballor and Stephen J. Grabill. Grand Rapids, MI: Christian's Library Press, 2011.

Marshall, Paul A., Sander Griffioen, and Richard J. Mouw, eds. *Stained Glass: Worldviews and Social Science*. Lanham, MD: University Press of America, 1989.

Mouw, Richard. *He Shines in All That's Fair: Culture and Common Grace*. Grand Rapids, MI: Eerdmans, 2002.

Myers, Kenneth A. *All God's Children and Blue Suede Shoes: Christians and Popular Culture*. Westchester, IL: Crossway, 1989.

Naugle, David. *Worldview: The History of a Concept*. Grand Rapids, MI: Eerdmans, 2002.

Pearcey, Nancy. *Total Truth: Liberating Christianity from its Cultural Captivity*. Wheaton, IL: Crossway, 2004.

Ryken, Leland. *The Liberated Imagination: Thinking Christianly about the Arts*. Wheaton, IL: Harold Shaw, 1989.

———. *Worldly Saints: The Puritans as They Really Were*. Grand Rapids, MI: Zondervan, 1986.

Sire, James. *Naming the Elephant: Worldview as a Concept*. Downers Grove, IL: InterVarsity, 2004.

————. *The Universe Next Door: A Basic Worldview Catalog*, 5th ed. Downers Grove, IL: IVP Academic, 2009.

Smith, James K. A. *Desiring the Kingdom: Worship, Worldview, and Cultural Formation*. Cultural Liturgies, vol. 1. Grand Rapids, MI: Baker Academic, 2009.

Treier, Daniel J., Mark Husbands, and Roger Lundin, eds. *The Beauty of God: Theology and the Arts*. Downers Grove, IL: InterVarsity, 2007.

Turnau, Ted. *Popologetics: Popular Culture in Christian Perspective*. Phillipsburg, NJ: P&R, 2012.

Walsh, Brian, and Richard Middleton. *The Transforming Vision: Shaping a Christian World View*. Downers Grove, IL: InterVarsity, 1984.

Wenther, David, and Mark D. Linville, eds. *Philosophy and the Christian Worldview: Analysis, Assessment and Development*. Bloomsbury Studies in Philosophy of Religion. London: Bloomsbury Academic, 2012.

Wolters, Albert M. *Creation Regained: Biblical Basics for a Reformational Worldview*, 2nd ed. Grand Rapids, MI: Eerdmans, 2005.

GENERAL INDEX

SCRIPTURE INDEX